Inspecting the Inspectorate

Inspecting the Inspectorate
Ofsted Under Scrutiny

Kevin Avison, Tim Benson,
Mick Brookes, Sarah Drake,
Graham Lester George,
John MacBeath, Warwick Mansell,
Bavaani Nanthabalan,
Pauline Perry,
Anastasia de Waal (ed.)

Civitas: Institute for the Study of Civil Society
London
Registered Charity No. 1085494

First Published November 2008

© Civitas 2008
77 Great Peter Street
London SW1P 2EZ
Civitas is a registered charity (no. 1085494)
and a company limited by guarantee, registered in
England and Wales (no. 04023541)

email: books@civitas.org.uk

ISBN 978-1-906837-00-6

Independence: Civitas: Institute for the Study of Civil Society is a registered educational charity (No. 1085494) and a company limited by guarantee (No. 04023541). Civitas is financed from a variety of private sources to avoid over-reliance on any single or small group of donors.

All publications are independently refereed. All the Institute's publications seek to further its objective of promoting the advancement of learning. The views expressed are those of the authors, not of the Institute.

Typeset by
Civitas

Printed in Great Britain by
Hartington Litho Ltd
Lancing, Sussex

Contents

Authors

Kevin Avison, Executive officer, Steiner Waldorf Schools Fellowship. Kevin Avison has taught in maintained and Steiner schools. He is an executive officer to the Steiner Waldorf Schools Fellowship and co-coordinator and senior adviser to the Steiner Waldorf Advisory Service. He has two grown-up children educated in Waldorf schools.

Tim Benson, Head teacher. Tim Benson has been a head teacher at three primaries over a period of 22 years in increasingly large schools. His present school in East Ham is one of the largest in the country with nearly 900 pupils.

Mick Brookes, General Secretary, National Association of Head Teachers (NAHT). The NAHT has more than 28,000 school leaders in primary, secondary and special education. It is the largest union of its kind in Europe and the second largest in the world. An experienced teacher and head, Mick Brookes joined the NAHT Council in 1995 and was National President in 2000. He was elected General Secretary of the NAHT in April 2005.

Sarah Drake, Inspector. A former lay inspector, Sarah Drake has been a schools' inspector since 1993. Over the years she has been involved in more than 400 inspections. Under the current inspection regime, 'section 5', Drake has led over 60 Ofsted inspections.

Graham Lester George, Parent. Graham Lester George is a writer for film, television and radio. For three years he was Chair of the Writers' Guild of Great Britain, is currently Vice President of the European Writers' Congress and is also a member of Bafta. He is married and has four children, two of whom are still at school, and has been a governor at his youngest son's school. In 2006 he led a 'Parents' Action Group' to protest against Ofsted's judgement of one of his children's primary schools.

John MacBeath, Educationalist, University of Cambridge. John MacBeath is Chair of Educational Leadership at the University of Cambridge and Director of Learning. Until 2000 he was Director of the Quality in Education Centre at the University of Strathclyde in Glasgow. As well as focusing on leadership in his research, for the last decade Professor MacBeath has worked with schools, education authorities and national governments on school self-evaluation.

Warwick Mansell, Education journalist and author. Warwick Mansell is a senior reporter with the *Times Educational Supplement* (TES) and author of *Education by Numbers: the Tyranny of Testing*, published by Politico's. A reporter with the TES since 1999, Mansell has specialised in most areas of education, including Ofsted, teachers' unions and the politics of schooling. Since 2003, he has been the TES's testing and curriculum specialist.

Bavaani Nanthabalan, Head teacher. Bavaani Nanthabalan is head teacher at Torriano Junior School in North London's Kentish Town. Torriano Junior is a medium-sized school with a high proportion of pupils from ethnic minority backgrounds and 46 per cent of pupils on free school meals. In December 2005, Torriano Junior School was one of the first schools to be inspected within the newly introduced 'section 5' inspection regime. Ofsted judged the school to be 'outstanding'.

Pauline Perry, Former Her Majesty's Chief Inspector of Schools. Appointed to Her Majesty's Inspectorate of Schools in 1970, Pauline Perry was promoted to Staff Inspector in 1975. In 1981 she was made Chief Inspector, professional adviser to the Secretary of State on higher education, teacher policies and international relations. Today Baroness Perry is co-Chair of both the Conservative Party Policy Commission on Public Services and the all-party Parliamentary Universities Group.

Anastasia de Waal, Director of Family and Education at Civitas. A social policy analyst, she is also a qualified primary school teacher, trained specifically for teaching in the inner city. De Waal is author of *Inspection, Inspection, Inspection* (2006) and *Second Thoughts on the Family* (2008), as well as a number of reports on education. She is a regular contributor to print and broadcast media, panellist for the *Observer* and board member of Women's Parliamentary Radio.

Editor's Note

It should be noted that the views of the contributors are not necessarily reflected in pieces other than their own.

Foreword

It is refreshing to read a series of such knowledgeable and thoughtful essays that shed so much light on the current schools inspection system and the role of Ofsted.

Over the past 20 years we have seen governments become increasingly concerned with identifying ways in which school standards can be raised. To achieve this we have seen a proliferation of measures, from the introduction of a now daunting system of testing and assessment through to the strong reliance on the inspection of schools. Such mechanisms of account-ability and school quality are found in many countries, but it is England that stands out above most in terms of the intensity of its testing and assessment regime and the influence of its inspection services.

Who can now believe that the Department of Education, now the DCSF, was traditionally viewed as a marginal office? It is presently considered to be one of the most distinguished ministries for ambitious poli-ticians. Power and responsibility once rested at a local authority level and testing, inspection and curriculum once resided in the hands of local education authorities. Perhaps it was a bright civil servant who had perused the *One Minute Manager* asserting 'if you can't measure it you can't manage it' that changed all of this; published in 1984, it was perhaps the former Secretary of State Ken Baker who drew most influence from it.

The fundamental issue currently within education policy is to find the most accurate, valid and just way in which to measure schools' achievement. At present we have a schools system in which we test at 7, 11,

14, 16, 17 and 18, though, as from summer 2009 there will be no more testing at 14. The government may introduce even more regular testing through single level tests. Increasingly the tests and the associated school performance tables dominate the educational landscape. Accountability is necessary, but many of us fear that teaching to the test can prevent students from accessing a rich and varied curriculum and can distort effective teaching and learning.

There is overwhelming evidence to suggest that the present inspection regime is consistent with our reliance on the quantifiable. Recently Ofsted's inspection process has become shorter and is euphemistically referred to as 'the lighter touch'. Many people believe that more attention should be paid to inspection reports than to the results of the key stage tests or GCSE and A level results, yet, as inspection reports and results become increasingly interchangeable, many educational practitioners feel that the inspectors' minds are made up long before they observe the quality of teaching or the atmosphere within a school.

This collection of essays represents the voices of those who have a genuine understanding of, and experience in, our schools and who believe that the excellent teaching and learning that exists can be jeopardised if care is not taken to ensure the right balance between accountability through testing and inspection on the one hand and a stimulating and rich curriculum on the other.

Barry Sheerman MP, Chairman of the Children, Schools and Families Select Committee

Introduction

Anastasia de Waal[*]

In 2007, Barry Sheerman, chair of the Education and
Skills Select Committee, and I co-chaired a seminar in
the House of Commons on what was working in
Ofsted's (the Office for Standards in Education)
inspections—and what was not. The aim of the seminar
was to collect a broad range of perspectives on Ofsted
inspection—including those of two head teachers, an
inspector and a Cambridge educationalist—in order to
formulate a picture of how well the existing inspection
regime was working. This report is an extension and
expansion of that seminar, bringing to print the views
of those who contributed to it, together with several
supplementary ones. The final collection here includes
a practising Ofsted inspector; a head teacher from a
school deemed by Ofsted to be 'outstanding'; a head
teacher from a struggling school; an academic
specialist on systems of school inspection; the general
secretary of a teachers' union; a parent whose child's
school was inspected under Ofsted's current 'section 5'
regime; a senior reporter for the *Times Educational
Supplement*; an executive from the Steiner Waldorf
Fellowship (a body that represents Steiner Waldorf
schools, which currently can only educate as

---

[*] **Anastasia de Waal** is Director of Family and Education at
Civitas and a qualified primary school teacher.

1

independent sector providers); and a former chief inspector who served under Ofsted's predecessor, Her Majesty's Inspectorate (HMI). Lending particular significance to the collection is the range of perspectives presented, and importantly, whilst we are more accustomed to hearing accounts of Ofsted from teachers, it is less frequently that we are privy to, as it were, views from the 'other side of the fence': the inspector and parent. Barry Sheerman's interest in the publication is of additional value, in that he is the long-serving chair of the one body to which Ofsted is accountable, the Children, Schools and Families Select Committee (formerly Education and Skills).

School inspection in England has undergone consid-erable change, both prior to and following the introduction of Ofsted. Preceding Ofsted's establish-ment in 1992, under John Major's government, school inspection was carried out by HMI. The move from HMI to Ofsted was a significant one, leading to a dramatic shift in the relationship between schools and the inspectorate (see former Her Majesty's Chief Inspector of Schools, Pauline Perry, chapter 4), with Ofsted adopting a considerably more forceful role. Since 1992, Ofsted itself has implemented considerable changes to its inspection regime: from how often schools are inspected, to the notice that they are given of an inspection, to how long the inspection lasts and what is inspected. The inspection regime for maintained schools has thus shifted from schools being inspected on average every six years, with six to ten weeks' notice, to being inspected on average every three years, with around two days' notice. Ofsted has also narrowed its inspection remit within schools, whilst concurrently widening its overall remit to include additional educational providers. As such, under the auspices of 'shorter, sharper'—and crucially cheaper—'section 5' inspections, school inspections are now no longer 'subject' level, meaning that individual curriculum subjects are no longer specifically scrutinised during school inspection. Instead schools are judged chiefly on their performance data—their test and exam scores—and what is referred to as their 'self-evaluation'. Meanwhile, 'children's services, schools, colleges, initial teacher training, work-based learning and adult education are now included in Ofsted's remit.'[1] Accordingly, Ofsted is now the 'Office for Standards in Education, Children's Services and Skills', meaning that, as Ofsted puts it: 'at least one in every three people use the services we inspect or regulate across education, children's services and skills'.[2]

The question is: how are Ofsted's school inspections regarded by those on whom they impact? Whilst some improvements are thought to have been made to Ofsted inspection in recent years, there continue to be perceived weaknesses—which by many are seen to constitute fundamental flaws. That there is room for improvement in the inspection regime is something which Ofsted itself recognises, evident not least from its recent consultation in which a range of proposals for changes to school inspection from 2009 were presented. The key proposals are as follows: a 'proportionate' system of inspection whereby schools that are doing less well (with success determined largely by test and exam results) are inspected more frequently; giving schools no notice of inspections; more time spent observing lessons during inspection; and enabling parents to 'call up' an inspection if they are concerned about a school and an inspection is not imminently due. Ofsted is also proposing that inspectors be shadowed by the senior management team, with the purpose of helping the school to understand how judgements have been arrived at; and finally, Ofsted is proposing that new standards, in the form of performance data, be attached to inspection grades. With the exception of more lesson observation, these proposals leave unaddressed many of the issues which currently hinder effective inspection; and worse still, in some cases—notably the greater emphasis on exam and test results—exacerbate them.

Whilst there are significant differences between the contributors' accounts of inspection, in spite of the variety of perspectives, two common themes emerge. The first is a feeling that there are elemental problems within the current school inspection regime. Whilst there are generally thought to be at least some positive aspects within Ofsted inspection, on the whole there is a greater emphasis on what is currently problematic. Given that the contributors' remit was to review 'what is working well in school inspection and what is not', this imbalance rather suggests that Ofsted is getting it more wrong than right. The second theme which emerges through the chapters is that Ofsted's school inspection regime is not presenting a sufficiently clear picture of the quality of education in schools. As gauging the quality of provision is surely a key function of school inspection, this perceived weakness is clearly critical.

Criticism of Ofsted's school inspection is not new; since its inception, Ofsted has come under fire, with concern tending to focus on the notion that its approach was too 'draconian'. Ofsted continues to be considered unnecessarily punitive today; however, arguably of even greater concern now, is the detail of what is inspected.

A recurring point in the contributions is that the quality of the school, as it is gauged by Ofsted, hangs largely on how the school is performing in national examinations. As one head remarks in *Times Educational Supplement* reporter Warwick Mansell's chapter (p. 53), it is currently questionable as to whether there is any point in Ofsted inspectors visiting schools at all as performance data appears to determine their judgements. Several of the contributors—Tim Benson, Mick Brookes, Bavaani Nanthabalan, Graham Lester George and Warwick Mansell—complain of the emphasis on test and exam results. Graham Lester George writes about Ofsted from the perspective of a parent and it is interesting to connect his view of a focus on Sats results in primary school Ofsted inspections to a broader take on parents' view on the topic. There is quite a lot of evidence to show that *teachers*, and educationalists more generally, do not feel that results present a well-rounded picture of school quality; significantly, despite their centrality within

5

education today, data also suggest that this is a view shared by parents. According to some recent survey evidence on Key Stage 2 Sats, for example, two-thirds of parents think that these tests are a waste of time.[3] Notably, however, with a system of inspection whereby quality is heavily determined by performance data, parents may well find themselves *inadvertently* putting results as top priority. Judging by the fact that many estate agents now link their properties to local schools' Ofsted reports, parents do consider inspection judgements to be important indicators of school quality. In light of Ofsted's emphasis on exam data, this ultimately means that parents who take heed of Ofsted's judgements are, consciously or not, attaching a significant weight to results.

One primary reason for doubting the value of performance data is based on a common scepticism about whether test and exam results can truly convey the whole picture of provision. In the case of primary school results this is particularly so as only maths, English and science are tested. Primary head teacher in East London's Newham, Tim Benson (chapter 2), conveys this issue pertinently in his contribution. He describes the inspectors' disinterest in those activities which did not feature in Ofsted's result-focused remit. Yet Benson's observations illustrate that the aspects of a school outside the gaze of Ofsted should not only be taken into account, but may in fact be *more* reliable indicators of school quality than results. Benson exemplifies this point by describing the way in which his school was judged to be effective on the basis of essentially a better-performing cohort whereas had the school been inspected the previous year the same quality of provision would have likely been judged to be inadequate.

The issue with exam results in this country has however extended from concerns about their limitations as gauges of school quality, to an active distrust of results, largely in view of a 'teaching to the test' pandemic which even Her Majesty's Chief Inspector of Schools, Christine Gilbert, has acknowledged.[4] The *Times Educational Supplement's* Warwick Mansell, (p. 55) presents the evidence for the problem of Ofsted's reliance on data on the basis that they are 'vulnerable to manipulation'. That school inspection judgements are therefore based on a potentially very questionable foundation, strongly suggests that the inspection judgements themselves are questionable.

With results already of central importance in the English education system today, the danger when inspection judgements also rest on them is that they become the sum of education quality and therefore the only goal. Bearing in mind the issues surrounding test and exam results, this is seriously jeopardising definitions of quality and thereby the pursuit of higher standards in schools, as well as increasing the likelihood of schools resorting to manipulating their results. Ofsted's proposals for 2009 would very likely exacerbate this situation. Firstly, as results become *more* central to inspection judgements, if, as proposed, minimum results are attached to each inspection judgement grade: 'We will set indicators which define minimum standards for learners' outcomes, such as Key Stage 2 results and the proportion of learners gaining five A*-C grades at GCSE, including English and mathematics.'[5] Secondly, with a more 'proportionate' system of inspection whereby schools doing less well (with success determined largely by results) are inspected more frequently.

The second contentious way in which school quality is gauged in the current Ofsted inspection regime is through self-evaluation. Whilst it is not in fact statutory, schools are strongly 'encouraged' to complete a 'self-evaluation form' (SEF). Judging by the centrality of the SEF in inspection, there is strong reason to believe that a school which fails to produce a completed self-evaluation form would suffer consequences.

In principle the SEF remedies many of Ofsted's current weaknesses by making inspection more collaborative, giving schools the opportunity to communicate their strengths and weaknesses and identify the areas in which they need further improvement. However, whilst self-evaluation has, again in principle, been welcomed by the education community, its realisation has been a disappointment to many, and entailed a series of new problems. Professor John MacBeath (chapter 3) has spent many years researching systems of self-evaluation. In his contribution he argues that the problem with Ofsted's self-evaluation is that it is much more akin to self *regulation*. Unlike successful self-evaluation models which are school-driven organic processes that motivate and improve schools, the Ofsted model is top-down, rigid, laborious and a potential hindrance to schools. Schools do not have 'ownership' of the self-evaluation process, rather they are forced to standardise themselves to fit into a tick-box chart. There are also concerns on a practical level; as head teacher Bavaani Nanthabalan (chapter 6) notes, echoing evidence from the National Foundation for Educational Research,[6] completing the self-evaluation form is hugely time-consuming for schools.

Ofsted's dependence on the SEF is highlighted in inspector Sarah Drake's contribution (chapter 1). The shortness of the section 5 inspection schedule means that inspectors are reliant on schools collating a 'profile' of the school through the self-evaluation form. Both the number of inspectors and how long they spend in schools have been significantly scaled down in the section 5 inspection regime; even more so in Ofsted's 'reduced tariff inspections'. As Drake points out, it is therefore imperative that schools have the data ready for the inspector as the time which the inspectors are able to spend on inspection is so limited. With this in mind, the 'optional' element of the self-evaluation form is clearly misleading: inspection is designed around the SEF as former Her Majesty's Chief Inspector of Schools (HMCI), David Bell made plain when section 5 inspections were introduced: 'Ofsted can then focus its inspection on the school's evaluation of itself and therefore make inspection sharper and more helpful.'[7]

9

It was again former HMCI David Bell who predicted another of the pitfalls of Ofsted's self-evaluation: 'We need to be careful that self-evaluation does not become an industry.'[8] Two things have contributed to bringing this about. Firstly, research suggests that the self-evaluation form does not necessarily 'capture' a school. Whilst the quality of self-evaluation is supposed to be a key indicator of the quality of a school's leadership,[9] it can instead be more indicative of how effectively the self-evaluation form has been completed. A study by Sara Bubb and Peter Earley published in 2008 brought out such problems with self-evaluation. One of the most significant (which feeds into the issue of shorter inspections) is that Ofsted does not always properly investigate 'claims' made by a school in the self-evaluation form; this could be problematic if a school is either excessively negative or positive about its provision. As one local authority representative is quoted as saying: 'In the current short inspection system, especially with less rigorous [inspection] teams, schools can definitely get rosier Ofsted reports as a result of a well-written self-evaluation that "bigs up" the school.'[10]

Secondly, self-evaluation has become quite literally an industry: private companies are cashing in on self-evaluation, at the expense of not just schools but also the taxpayer. Achieving a 'good' self-evaluation form may entail the deployment of private sector consultants. A significant number of private companies today provide tools and advice on 'how to do' self-evaluation successfully.[11] Tribal Education, one of the Regional

Inspection Service Providers which is contracted to provide Ofsted with additional inspectors, states in its training material for prospective inspectors that: 'There will clearly be schools looking for advisers from the private sector to guide them in preparing for inspection and completing their self-evaluation process.'[12]

Despite the heightened rhetorical importance of 'parent power', parents' views, as well as scope for inspectors' professional opinions, have been marginalised in the short inspection regime. Whereas previously parents were interviewed by inspectors during inspection, today the only inclusion of their views in the process is via a questionnaire. In the given period it can be difficult to ensure that parents fill it in, a frustration noted by head teacher Bavaani Nanthabalan. Ofsted's proposal to give parents greater say in the inspection process by enabling them to 'call up' an inspection is particularly notable in light of this simultaneous 'squeezing out' of their views. Aside from the fact that incorporating this mechanism suggests an inadequate inspection schedule, in which schools can survive as problematic unnoticed by Ofsted, giving parents greater say in inspections would be much better achieved by allowing more parental input within existing arrangements.

A recurring theme overall is that Ofsted is simply not doing an adequate job of inspecting schools. Countering the notion that schools are averse to scrutiny there is a pervasive feeling, extending beyond the report, that teachers actually want to be more *closely* inspected. It is common to hear teachers' disappointment at not being observed by inspectors while teaching, for example. Even pupils think that Ofsted is not getting to know their schools properly. While putting the report together I interviewed two pupils from a Hertfordshire secondary school in Bishop's Stortford about their views on school inspection. The girls, who were just finishing Year 7, had experienced an Ofsted inspection in their primary school the previous year. As with the other contributors, I was interested in whether, drawing from their personal experience, these pupils thought that inspection could be improved. In their opinion inspectors should look more closely at the school:

> The inspectors could come into assembly, for example, because that's when all the school are together. They could also talk more to the pupils, not just about work but whether they liked the school.[13]

Driving the 'shortening and sharpening' of inspection has been Ofsted's need to economise. Alongside the expansion of the services which it inspects, Ofsted has been set the target of significantly cutting its annual budget. As well as the issues raised so far there are other ways in which this economising is apparent in school inspection. For example, as well as even fewer inspectors taking part in Ofsted's cheapest form of school inspection, the reduced tariff inspections (see p. 23), specialist inspectors no longer carry out inspection on particular age groups. The effects of this cost-cutting measure is that inspectors are less well-qualified to gauge specific provision (for example for infants). Outsourcing inspection to Regional Inspection Service Providers (RISPs) has also been a way in which Ofsted has reduced its expenditure. The problem with this is that RISP inspectors are generally less well qualified.[14] Unsurprisingly schools are said to prefer inspections which are led by full-time Ofsted inspectors, known as HMIs. Unfortunately HMI-led inspections are in the minority.

A highly standardised, or to put it more colloquially, 'tick-box' approach to gauging quality is a prerequisite for inspectors who often have neither much time to spend in schools nor much training. With little time allowed for a thorough investigation of school provision, results become the definitive gauge of quality through necessity as much as through their prioritisation in education generally. Results which, as inspector Sarah Drake observes, can be more than a year out of date, demonstrate that even on their own terms the data used for Ofsted inspections are not necessarily reliable. Likewise, lack of time in school leaves inspectors dependent on schools presenting them with a picture of provision through the self-evaluation form.

It is clear that, for school inspection to be improved, the focus of inspection needs to be broadened and more resources need to be made available to the front line. For inspection to have any value—for inspectors to be able to identify how schools are really doing—the inspection regime must allow inspectors to get an in-depth look at provision.

Cheap, short and sharp inspection, whatever it may euphemistically be billed as, is by definition restricted to seeing only a superficial snapshot of school provision. Effective school inspection requires the resources for well-trained, professional inspectors who are able to spend periods in schools adequate for truly gauging the quality of provision. An inspection regime which is able to go even further and actually *aid* school improvement, should be the aim.

1

Inspection Today

Sarah Drake[*]

Under the former regime, according to the size of school, inspections could have up to 50 inspector days with up to 18 inspectors over four or five days. This meant that all subjects were looked at in depth; so, for example, an English inspector would observe each teacher teaching that subject at least twice. In other words, in the past, inspection was very thorough but also hugely time-consuming and expensive.

Today's inspection regime has been shortened considerably since it is looking at the establishment as an overall provider, rather than subjects individually. Under the current system, we have a maximum of five inspectors over two days. Essentially that translates as one and a half days, since the final afternoon on day two is taken-up with finalising the judgements and drafting the feedback.

Inspections are nevertheless still based around the same, if somewhat contracted, criteria. These criteria include standards and achievement; pupils' personal and social development as well as spiritual, moral, social and cultural development; the quality of

---

[*] Sarah Drake is writing in her role as a practising school inspector for Ofsted. The views expressed here are Drake's own rather than those of Ofsted.

15

teaching and learning; the curriculum; care, guidance and support; and leadership and management.

The big difference today is that the revised inspection schedule is very, very tight. The process begins with an examination of the school's self-evaluation form (SEF) as the starting point, along with its previous inspection report and its published data (exam and test results)—but we are all aware that statistics do not tell the whole story. We also talk with the head teacher during that initial period, generally for around an hour, about arrangements, timetables, planned teacher and pupil interviews and the documentation which will be needed. We have one day for primary schools, and two days for secondary schools, to use all this information to prepare what is called the 'pre-inspection briefing'. This document synthesises the available information, raises hypotheses and poses key questions that will set the inspection trails. Once this has all been done, we then have to arrange the team inspection plan and get the pre-inspection briefing to the school by email—all by around 3.30 p.m., the end of the school day.

The next part of the inspection starts on the second day for primary schools and the third day for secondary schools. We arrive at around eight o'clock, are given a tour of the school and meet the staff. Following that, the pre-inspection briefing is discussed with the head teacher. The remainder of the day is then spent observing lessons and other activities, specialist withdrawal groups for extra numeracy or literacy support or speech therapy, for example. During breaks

SARAH DRAKE

and lunchtime we talk to pupils, teaching assistants and support staff who supervise breaks, in order to ensure that child protection and health and safety procedures have been properly understood and are being implemented. We also hold discussions with the head teacher and senior management team to confirm the quality of leadership and management, and with pupils to gain their views of what the school is really like.

In secondary schools we may also talk to other staff but in primary schools this is usually after school hours because primary teachers have less flexible time during the day. We may also talk to parents and governors, as well as possibly the local authority representative, to find out more about the school. In addition, we look at documentation relating to, for example, safe recruitment of staff, pupils' progress, the school's monitoring of its provision and subsequent actions to bring about improvements. We also look at parental questionnaires to highlight any issues in the school. If the inspection is only for one day, inspectors also need time to finalise judgements and prepare the draft feedback to the school; if it is for two days, to make initial judgements and alert the school to any further evidence that may be needed on the second day.

The strengths of the section 5 inspection system

Some elements of the new section 5 inspection regime are both very welcome and working well. As inspection is intended to, the current system provides

17

an independent and up-to-date assessment of what is happening in schools. There is now far greater scope to inspect schools more often, which means that teachers are kept on their toes. In the school year 2006-2007, for example, 8,200 schools were inspected, meaning that within the current system topical information on around a third of all schools in the country is available at any one time. The shorter cycle also means that today no pupil will be left in a failing school for the entirety of their primary or secondary career.

Another advantage is that short notice inspections mean that schools prepare less paperwork and there is generally less disruption for teachers and pupils. Now schools are able to spend their time on what they should be doing—teaching—rather than preparing for Ofsted. Short notice also provides a clearer picture of the school 'as it is', warts and all. As well as being shorter and the notice period having been reduced, inspections now also have a much sharper focus. There is a very specific emphasis on pupils' achievement and the *impact* of the school's actions. This helps to clarify the effectiveness of the school's leadership rather than just its good intentions.

Self-evaluation is at the heart of the section 5 inspections. The emphasis on pupils' achievement has led to some improvements in schools' self-evaluation, although this is not always as focused as it should be. There is still a tendency for schools to write more about input—what the school does—rather than outcomes— the impact of the actions on pupils' learning and well-being. However one of the main benefits of self-evaluation is that the concept of inspecting *with* rather than *to* the school is much more apparent.

In addition, the increased frequency of inspection under section 5 may also help protect children by ensuring that safeguarding procedures are in place, which previously would have been solely reliant on local authority action.

Another new positive is the use of more practising school staff as inspectors. This is both liked by schools and brings the inspection team up-to-date awareness of the current demands on teachers. Furthermore, it is also good professional development for teachers.

When it comes to the actual reporting of the inspection judgements, in line with the slimmer inspection system, today's shorter reports are both much more accessible and sharper. A letter to pupils, about the judgements and how they can contribute to school improvement, is also included. Within the new regime there is now a maximum three-week turn-around for the report unless a school becomes a 'category' school i.e. is given a 'notice to improve' or put into 'special measures' in which case, due to the extensive moderation procedures, publication takes a further two weeks. For those schools that do go into categories, regular termly monitoring is followed by an early re-inspection, which helps to ensure improvement.

Under the terms of the revised reduced tariff inspections, being piloted since September 2007, we are working even more closely with the schools to reach provisional agreement on judgements from analysis of the published data and self-evaluation form evidence. This is making the job for inspectors more manageable —these inspections involve one inspector for one day unless the school has more than 900 pupils—however it could lead to things not being picked up.

The weaknesses

Some elements of the current inspection system are less successful.

Although the shorter inspection schedule has benefits, as outlined, the tightness of the schedule is potentially difficult. If all goes according to plan, the current process is manageable, but any spanner in the works, however small, can be fundamentally problematic. For example, if the school does not submit its self-evaluation form in a timely fashion (something which is increasingly common as schools become more used to the system and wait until after the notifying phone call to finalise their SEF) it is very difficult for the lead inspector to have then assimilated all the information necessary prior to his or her initial phone call to the school.

Another issue relates to the timeliness of publication of formal assessment data. Validated exam and test data are central to the inspection team's information gathering. Delays in getting validated statistical data about Sats, GCSE and other test results mean that what we are using can be up to 16 to 18 months out of date. For example, in October 2007 there was no validated data relating to tests taken in 2007 so we had to work with 2006 data. Similarly, information about the 2006 key stage 3 tests was not available until well into 2007—almost a whole year later. Given the emphasis now on 'value-added'—i.e. how much progress pupils have made in a key stage—this proves very difficult for the inspection process.

Another drawback of the shortness of the inspection process is that we rely greatly on schools having adequate systems for assessing and monitoring pupils' progress. If the school does not analyse its own assessment and tracking information effectively then a huge amount of time is needed for the inspection team to do so. However that time is not available. As a result, if a school cannot provide this information, either other areas are skated over or the inspectors' judgements are based on incomplete information. (Of course, if such data is unavailable, this does raise questions over the quality of leadership and management and what the school bases its self-evaluation on.)

An additional issue is that the foundation subjects have lost emphasis in the section 5 inspection regime. The focus is now on English and maths and, to an extent, science and ICT. Because the section 5 regime is not a 'subject standards' inspection it means that inevitably other subjects can slip unnoticed. This emphasises to schools that these are the areas to concentrate on rather than encouraging a wider, more imaginative use of, for example, drama and art as a stimulus for writing.

Time constraints also mean that there are now very few lesson observations. The problem with this is that the small number of lessons seen—particularly as a proportion of lessons taught in large secondary schools—can mask the normal quality of teaching that pupils experience. The emphasis on outcomes, i.e. pupils' achievement, is understandable but a good evidence base of observations is necessary in order to diagnose any weaknesses, such as slow pace or lack of probing questioning, that might lead to pointers for improvement.

For Year 11, 12 and 13 lessons the section 5 regime poses an added issue. Inspecting secondary schools after May means that Year 11 and 13 students will definitely be absent and very likely Year 12 also—so judgements can be made having seen no lessons and having interviewed no students. This did not happen under section 10 (the previous regime) because no secondary inspections were carried out towards the end of the summer term.

Generally, the short, sharp section 5 regime means that there is now little room for inspectors to identify the detail of how schools could improve. Reduced time means that it is not always possible to unearth the real problems, for example, what makes the school 'only' satisfactory. Equally, there is little opportunity to provide any guidance for schools and spread good practice, things which definitely used to happen under section 10.

Relating to the move away from a focus on actual teaching, section 5 places great emphasis on liaison with the head teacher and senior management team. This means less time for discussion with other teachers, something which in the past was so revealing. The limited time span also means that it is no longer possible to build the levels of trust amongst teachers that, under section 10, led to greater frankness. Inspectors are now ever more reliant on the head teacher—which can be fine if they are professional, open and honest.

The short inspection period also means that, more generally, discussion with others involved in the school is minimised. There is currently little opportunity to gauge the views of parents or carers, pupils, workplace employers and colleges, for example, which in the past were so informative and often raised important queries. This is curious given the increasing emphasis on work-based learning and placements and, in many other walks of life such as the NHS, on stakeholder involvement.

Given that the emphasis is on the school as a whole rather than provision in separate subjects, there are now generic inspectors, trained to work in schools catering for pupils aged from three to 18. This is having the effect of diluting the specialist knowledge which in the past was so useful for schools.

Furthermore, the reduced tariff—i.e. number of inspector days—for inspections inevitably leads to inspectors working more in isolation. There is much less opportunity now to bounce ideas off colleagues, which can have an adverse impact on judgements. This is particularly so if you are inspecting a small school on your own or conducting a reduced tariff inspection (RTI).

There is a risk that RTIs are compromising the credibility of inspections. The tendency for these types of inspection is towards agreeing with the school lest disagreement should lead to a complaint that minimal evidence was collected. RTIs also reduce the opportunity for identifying, celebrating and disseminating good practice. From an initial 20 per cent of schools whose test data indicated they were highly successful, RTIs are now carried out in around 30 per cent of schools and the proportion is set to increase. Inevitably, this means that more 'satisfactory' schools will be inspected this way, allowing even less time for the inspection to identify the most important areas for improvement to help them become 'good' or better. RTIs may be cheaper, but the value for money is questionable.

In conclusion, there is a real time shortage for inspectors within the new inspection regime. Thoroughness is imperative for sound inspection judgements. The need to ensure this extends the inspectors' working day greatly because often there are simply not enough hours in the school day to ensure everything is covered in sufficient detail.

The way ahead

The most important change which needs to be made is the provision of a more realistic time allowance for an inspection. HMIs (Her Majesty's Inspectors, Ofsted's full-time inspectors) clearly recognise this. For example, on inspections led by them, there is sometimes a supernumerary HMI inspector who is 'training' but magically carries out extra work, such as data analysis, note-taking or interviewing. On HMI-led reduced tariff inspections, they also have the opportunity to run them from afternoon to afternoon, i.e. still within the 24 hours that constitutes the 'day' tariff for an RTI but allowing the evening for reflection and data analysis of data. Regional Inspection Service Providers have however tendered to Ofsted for a daily tariff for each inspection and self-employed Additional Inspectors are paid a daily rate. This means that, for them, the time scale has no such flexibility because it would cost more money.

Another area for improvement is the timeliness of the availability of the data on which inspectors base their judgements—the national result statistics and school self-evaluation forms.

There is also a need for some more detailed inspections, including a greater emphasis on the foundation subjects. If more money is not available, perhaps some more closely tailored inspections could be introduced where certain elements become the focus for specific schools. Similarly, in-depth sampling of schools in a local area could be introduced whereby inspections concentrated on specific areas, such as a subject or the progress of specific groups, as identified through data analysis. There has been talk of a longer period between inspections. This would definitely not be welcome. If a school has 'got away with it' as 'satisfactory', pupils should not have to endure weak provision for a longer period. This would only reduce equality of opportunity and is also likely to induce more disaffection among pupils.

To conclude, at its best, inspection is an art, not a science. As in every walk of life this requires skilled practitioners to achieve the best outcomes and also a realistic timescale in which to do so.

2   Head Teacher Vulnerability In Challenging Schools

Tim Benson[*]

I have been teaching for 30 years, the last 25 of those in tough areas of East London; 22 of those as a head teacher, in three different primary schools. My present school, where I have been for ten years, is one of the largest primary schools in the country with nearly 900 pupils on its roll. Situated in East Ham, it serves an extremely diverse and mobile population. Currently, 95 per cent of the population is from an assorted mixture of ethnicities, with many children from Sri Lanka, Africa, India, Pakistan and more recently, Eastern Europe. Forty-three languages are spoken in the school and a number of children are now learning in their third or fourth language, having settled in another European country before reaching England. I moved to East London 25 years ago as I had a passionate desire to live and work with those communities most in need. All these years later I am still driven by that passion and a desire for equality of opportunity and provision.

Whilst at the Labour Party conference at Bournemouth in 2007, I had the opportunity to speak to Ed Balls, Secretary of State for Children, Schools and Families, who told me that he had not been aware that

---

[*]   Tim Benson is writing in his role as a head teacher.

Ofsted was a verb; he also graciously accepted that as a new Secretary of State he had much to learn. I have had the interesting experience of being 'Ofsteded' five times. There from the beginning, I have had the opportunity to watch the beast grow and then reduce in size periodically, stretching its limbs during its metamorphosis. On each of the five occasions that the inspection team has descended, the inspectors have behaved in a very professional manner and I have worked hard, as have my leadership teams, to ensure a positive outcome. However, in truth, the inspection teams have told me very little about my school that I did not already know and the outcome on each occasion has been primarily that the school knew where it was in terms of development, and what it needed to do to take the next part of its journey. From discussion with many colleagues throughout the country, that seems to have been the case for the vast majority of inspections. One certainly felt at the early stages that it was a colossally expensive exercise (seven inspectors in for a week) to tell you that you were doing OK.

Each time inspectors have visited they have come with a very different agenda and one has had to learn the new rules of the game to ensure the appropriate response and outcome. Easy to do when the rules are available before you start to play. The smaller teams, the less lengthy inspection and the shorter notice of inspection are all moves that I support and feel have improved the experience from a schools' point of view — certainly mine. However, and this is a huge reservation no matter how pleasant and professional our colleagues from the inspection teams have been, there has been a very strong perception that the system is punitive and designed to try to catch schools out. There are high hurdles that had to be jumped and failure to do so would have serious consequences.

The most recent incarnation of inspection is rightly focusing on those schools that are underachieving in terms of their comparative national data. My school and many others like it—the tough schools, the challenging schools, the very schools where the children get a rough ride anyway, in terms of housing and social deprivation—are potentially very vulnerable to this concentration on arbitrary sets of data and targets. I know some schools do very well in these circumstances—I have been a head in one of them two years ago—however I have also been a head of a school that was struggling: my present one.

One morning, in my present school, a parent ran across the playground to me, clutching his copy of the *Sun* newspaper. 'Mr Benson, Mr Benson,' he cried, 'You are one of the best schools in the country.' Feeling sure I could trust the professional integrity of the nation's favourite newspaper I turned to the central double page spread. 'Top Fifty Schools in the Country', proclaimed the headline, and sure enough there we were, Nelson Primary School, 36th in the country. But regrettably, there is a contextualisation that you need: we had not achieved the best literacy or numeracy results; we had reached our place at the top of the tables by eating more Walkers' crisps than nearly any other school in the country and earned ourselves free books. No matter that with 900 pupils matters were balanced in our favour—or that many parents worked the night shift at the local Tesco's and had managed to acquire sufficient available stocks for their offspring.

Our actual results in literacy and numeracy were worryingly low two years ago. Not through indiscipline however (at the time I was on Sir Alan Steer's committee and helped to produce the report 'Learning Behaviour' for the then Schools Minister Jacqui Smith); not through a lack of hard work by my team of teachers and support staff; not because there wasn't a will to do better, to succeed, to try harder; not for lack of a ten-year commitment to developing community cohesion in a fluid and rapidly moving school population. Purely because, as happens in our most deprived areas, a set of circumstances were against us in the roller coaster ride that is life in challenging urban areas. For several years earlier we had faced severe teacher shortages and had had chronic recruitment difficulties. We had a huge mobility situation with 60 per cent of children moving on between Year 2 and Year 6 and 25 per cent of Year 6 were new during that year. What hope of achieving meaningful targets in those circumstances? When Ofsted came, I managed to find nine children who had been with us from start to finish; *nine* children—one per cent of our intake. Fortunately they had made progress.

We were actually 'Ofsteded' in the Autumn term of 2006, and we were described as a 'rapidly improving school' having had one set of improved results followed by, I am pleased to say, an even better set the following year. However, if we had had our inspection 12 months earlier I have no doubt that we would have been put into an Ofsted category. I have no doubt that many staff would have left, further compounding the problems. I have no doubt that I would have had the local authority visit where my future would have been discussed. I also have no doubt that my career would have been over.

What incentive is there for aspiring heads to take on these challenging schools? Like the football manager vulnerable to the run of bad games, we are dispensed with—to be replaced by whom? I recently worked with John MacBeath and John Howson on a project for the National College for School Leadership. Our report, 'Leading Appointments', identified the difficulties of recruitment to our most vulnerable schools.

I believe that if Ofsted has a place in the future it must be seen far less in terms of the sword of Damocles. We need a change of culture that is supportive and challenging, like the best practice that we see in our schools; encouraging schools and their staffs to do better, but also understanding the context of where they are in their development. We need to produce a judgement not solely based on a set of questionable data.

Last year during our inspection I forced our team to attend my school orchestra rehearsal; 60 children all playing orchestral instruments. The children told of how they were to sing—we have a splendid choir too at Nelson Primary School—at the Festival Hall and the Excel Centre. Other children reported coming top of Newham's school football league. Not one word on sport or music was included in our final inspection report.

Having lived through Ofsted, in all its transformations, it is failing, in my view, in that it still appears to be destructive where it should be constructive. It currently helps to create a culture of fear in our most vulnerable schools: the very schools that need the most encouragement and support.

3   A New Relationship with Schools?

John MacBeath*

Quality assurance systems around the world are in a state of continuous evolution. This is because no country has yet found the ideal balance between internal and external evaluation of school quality and effectiveness. At the two extremes are the view a) that only a rigorous external and objective system can provide an authentic picture of how good a school is, and b) that schools themselves are the only bodies that have the self-knowledge and expertise to evaluate themselves. Most commentators and policy bodies now believe that the ideal is a combination of the two and that external evaluation works best when there is strong self-evaluation in place, supported and challenged by external support sensitive to the school's context and unique circumstances. A 2004 study conducted by the Standing International Conference on Inspection in Europe found that:

> The school visits conducted as part of the project have shown that self-evaluation is most effective in countries that have the strongest external support to the process and thus have created a culture and climate for effective school self-evaluation.[1]

---

* John MacBeath is writing in his capacity as an academic specialist on systems of school inspection.

This was the rationale for the 'New Relationship with Schools' in England, a tacit admission that the old relationship had done more to damage than to improve schools.

A fairly substantial body of evidence is highly critical with regard to Ofsted's impact on improvement. Cullingford and Daniels' 1999[2] study reported an adverse effect on examination performance for a sample of schools, although it was dismissed by the then Chief Inspector of Schools, Chris Woodhead, as 'deeply flawed, ineptly executed and poorly argued'.[3] Rosenthal's study in the following year, however, also found 'a significant negative effect of Ofsted visits on school exam performance in the year of the inspection':

> Ofsted visits seem to have adverse effects on the standards of exam performance achieved by schools in the year of the Ofsted inspection. Perhaps the efforts required by teaching staff in responding to the demands of the school inspection system are great enough to divert resources from teaching so as to affect pupil achievement in the year of the visit. [4]

Employment of inspection consultants and rehearsal for the forthcoming event had become an increasingly common feature of school life. A report by Brunel University referred to 'anticipatory dread', impairing normal school development work and effectiveness of teaching, an impact on a school which, it was claimed, could last for over a year.[5]

In Hertfordshire, a group of secondary students conducted their own study of inspection and reported a tenser relationship with their teachers, special lessons being rehearsed beforehand and students and teachers having to be constantly 'on show' ever ready for the inspectors' visit.[6] 'Trouble students' were sent away to an outdoor pursuits centre to partake in a week-long-alternative education programme. Students also wrote: 'Teachers are too busy being stressed'; 'Some of them have no time to teach, they are so busy getting ready'; 'Everyone is telling us what to say and how to act. What is this dictatorship? Are we expecting Stalin or Hitler next week?'[7]

Such reactions are to be expected in systems where inspection carries high-stakes consequences for teachers. While Ofsted's strap-line was at one time 'Improvement through Inspection' (it is currently, in 2008, 'Raising Standards, Improving Lives'), ex-Chief Inspector David Bell (now Permanent Secretary at the Department for Children, Schools and Families) was ready to admit that inspection does not of itself improve schools:

> I have always been cautious in saying that inspection causes improvement because, frankly, we don't. But it has to be an important part of our thinking about inspection. You do try to understand what contribution inspection can make to improvement and that is a statutory base of the organisation. It forces us to be more articulate and explicit about that.
>
> To say inspection causes improvement is fundamentally unprovable. I think there are examples of where you have greater evidence of improvement being brought about by inspection, but again it's still not quite the same as saying it causes it. For example, our monitoring of schools with special measures is not causing improvement but most head teachers say to us that the process of professional debate and discussion with HMI brings some real bite to the improve-

ment process. I think it's a bit too simplistic to say that either Ofsted does cause improvement or Ofsted doesn't cause improvement.[8]

Ofsted's own analysis in 2004 found that in some cases inspected schools made greater progress than those that were not inspected and in other cases they didn't. Ofsted commented that 'there is little significance to be read into this except to say that inspection is neither a catalyst for instant improvement in GCSE results nor a significant inhibitor'.[9]

Ouston and Davies' 1998 study may go some way towards explaining the difference. Schools which were most positive about the inspection experience were those that did not allow the process to intimidate them because staff had a high level of professional self-confidence, enough to challenge the findings of the inspection teams. These schools were able to make their own professional judgements as to what was right for their school and welcomed the engagement in constructive dialogue with an outside team. There was already in these schools an incipient, or well-developed, self-evaluation culture.[10]

The New Relationship with Schools (NRwS as it has come to be known) was described by the then Schools Minister, David Miliband, as a covenant with schools: 'A new relationship with schools that will give schools the time, support and information they need to focus on what really matters.'[11] This may have ignited hope among school leaders that they would be released from the constraining effects of performance tables, government targets and inspection reports made public.

However, in the years following the Miliband speech there has been little evidence to suggest that a focus on what really matters has been realised in policy or in practice.

At the very heart of the new relationship are four key framing values: trust, support, challenge and net-working. The implication is that a 'New Relationship' has to be founded on these and cannot work unless they are in place. But what do these humpty-dumpty words mean? What, for example, is implied by the word 'trust', a precept on which all other consid-erations rest? Should it be taken to mean that teachers trust the goodwill of Ofsted's intentions? That teachers can trust that inspectors will be fair? Can it be taken to mean that the government trusts the professionalism and integrity of teachers? Or that inspectors trust the integrity and honesty of the school's own self-evaluation? Few, if any, of these are realistic aspir-ations given the asymmetry of the power relations between inspectors and schools.

The Dutch academic Leeuw argues for the impor-tance of reciprocity, the 'me-to-you-too' principle.[12] In other words, if external inspectors are to make judge-ments about school or classroom practice, professional principles require that they be mutual, negotiated and shared on an equal basis. However friendly the rhetoric, the bottom line was clearly articulated by David Miliband. Accountability drives everything. 'Without accountability there is no legitimacy; without legitimacy there is no support; without support there are no resources; and without resources there are no services.'[13] It is within this political imperative that school leaders and inspection teams have to negotiate, exploring where trust resides, what it means and how it is tested.

The introduction of the self-evaluation form (the SEF), however, has reinforced a conception of self-evaluation as a major, and often disruptive, event rather than an ongoing seamless process. In a series of workshops conducted for the National College for School Leadership involving 400 head teachers, completing the SEF in anticipation of inspection was interpreted by all but a handful of those present as mandatory, despite clarity in the guidelines that schools could use their own approaches. It was a brave and unusual head who did not hurry to complete the SEF in anticipation of an unexpected arrival of the Ofsted team. The brave and risk-taking head teachers, however, took Ofsted at its word—the SEF is *not* self-evaluation—and told their inquiry and improvement story in their own way.[14] These were heads of schools in which self-evaluation had a long and honourable history. It had grown and been nurtured over the years, attentive to students and teacher voice, grounded in continuing critical inquiry about learning and with reflective and critical feedback on the quality of teaching and leadership. But sadly, many of these home-grown initiatives had been overtaken by the Ofsted protocol, by a perceived need to work to a formula and a given set of indicators.

There is a compelling logic for systems with well-developed inspection regimes to devolve frameworks, process and criteria to schools themselves. With appropriate direction and requisite tools, schools can then conduct their own internal inspection. The paradox is, however, that the more governments provide the frameworks, indicators and tools, the less inventive and spontaneous the process at school and classroom level. Self-evaluation becomes a ritual event, a form of audit in which senior leaders assume the role of an internal inspectorate applying a set of common criteria.

In Table 3.1 (p. 40), self-evaluation is characterised by the right-hand side of the figure, centred on capacity building. It understands the iterative relationship between classroom life and school life, and between school learning and out-of-school learning. It recognises that students' learning and teachers' learning are integrally connected and that teachers' learning feeds from, and feeds into, organisational learning. It is this complexity and dynamic that is the missing ingredient in ritualised and formulaic approaches to self-evaluation, the box-ticking and form-filling that makes it such an onerous and tedious process for teachers and school leaders.

Grasping the complexity and dynamic of a school as a living growing entity is what Arnold Tomkins, a New York administrator, wrote about over a century ago:

> The organisation of the school must be kept mobile to its inner life. To one who is accustomed to wind up the machine and trust it to run for fixed periods, this constantly shifting shape of things will seem unsafe and troublesome. And

troublesome it is, for no fixed plan can be followed; no two schools are alike; and the same school is shifting, requiring constant attention and nimble judgement on the part of the school leader.[15]

Table 3.1
Self inspection and self-evaluation

Self-Inspection	Self-Evaluation
Top down	Bottom up
A one-off event	Is continuous and embedded in teachers' work
Provides a snapshot at a given time	Is a moving and evolving picture
Is time-consuming	Is time-saving
Is more about accountability than improvement	Is more about improvement than accountability
Applies a rigid framework	Is flexible and spontaneous
Uses a set of predetermined criteria	Uses, adapts and creates relevant criteria
Creates resistance	Engages and involves people
Can detract from learning and teaching	Improves learning and teaching
Encourages playing safe	Takes risks

Keeping a school mobile to its inner life is what self-evaluation is about, a continuing process of reflection which is implicit in the way people (teachers, students and administrators) think and talk about their work and what they do to make their practice explicit and discussable. Evidence from a number of countries leads to the same conclusion—schools that are able to take charge of change, rather than being controlled by it, are more effective and improve more rapidly than ones that are not.[16]

The importance of this was recognised by a Parliamentary sub-committee which reported in 1999.[17] It acknowledged the dysfunctions inherent in the Ofsted inspection and the stress it often caused to teachers. It recommended that the Chief Inspector 'should be concerned to improve morale and promote confidence in the teaching profession' and that inspectors should 'take account of self-evaluation procedures used by the school'. This demands a recasting of accountability, promoting an internal accountability which rests on mutual trust and a strong sense of collegiality.

The level or degree of internal accountability is measured by the degree of convergence among what individuals say they are responsible for (responsibility), what people say the organisation is responsible for (expectations), and the internal norms and processes by which people literally account for their work (accountability structures).[18] Without a strong sense of internal accountability, schools and teachers will always be subject to external pressures and remain reactive to externally driven change. They are more able to counteract the local, national and international forces at work when there is shared understanding of the difference between what they can and can't do, but continuously push at the boundaries of the possible. In the best schools change-forces arise from the inside, from a deeply rooted commitment to what is important and of lasting value.

4 From HMI to Ofsted

Pauline Perry*

It is common to hear heads and teachers of the over-40's generation, most commonly when their school has just experienced an Ofsted visit, wax nostalgic about the good old days of Her Majesty's Inspectorate (HMI), comparing Ofsted's ever-changing regimes with those of HMI. Are they just suffering from a misty memory of better times, or did HMI contribute to the system in a way that Ofsted has so far failed to do?

HMI did not, of course, disappear when Ofsted was set up in 1992. Although the numbers of HMIs (Her Majesty's Inspectors, under Her Majesty's Inspectorate) were much reduced, and the country-wide organisational structure was dismantled in favour of a centralised London-based headquarters, a small number of HMIs remained in HQ, though for much of the next decade the Chief Inspector was brought in from outside, and the role of HMI was greatly reduced.

A look at the organisation, established standard and ethos of HM Inspectorate, developed since 1839 and lasting until 1992, shall be our starting point for comparison with the 15-plus-year regime of Ofsted.

With very few exceptions, HMIs were recruited from the teaching profession. In the hard-fought com-

---

* Pauline Perry is writing in her role as former Chief Inspector of Schools under Her Majesty's Inspectorate.

petitions for appointment to the inspectorate, where hundreds of applications were received for every few advertised vacancies, appointees had to have success- ful and senior experience of the job they were to assess. Most were former heads or deputies; some came from colleges and university departments of education, and some from local authority inspectorate and adviser posts with solid teaching experience beforehand. They were appointed as full-time members of an inspect- orate of four to five hundred members, given a well- structured induction into the methodology of the work and traditions of HMI through several months of training and mentoring, and then assigned for their first four to five years to work in a particular area of the country, and with a particular specialist national team.

The geographical divisions, which covered up to ten local authorities in some areas, were overseen by a Divisional Inspector, who was responsible for the territorial assignment of responsibility of each HMI in her or his division. The specialist subject or 'phase' (age-group) assignment was the responsibility of a staff inspector with national responsibility for, say, history or mathematics, or early years, special education, secondary or teacher education, and so on.

Each team of specialists met regularly and worked together in inspection teams, developing standards for excellence in their subject or phase derived from the observation of many hundreds of lessons in their specialist field. It was by these standards that they formed their judgements of the work they observed in schools and colleges. Great care was taken to ensure that each individual HMI worked with different groupings of colleagues up and down the country, both in full inspections of individual schools and in specialist inspections of groups of schools, so that there was uniformity in standards of judgement, and 'group-think' by any small set of colleagues was avoided. Good practice seen in one school could be carried into others visited to help with each school's wish to provide good education to their pupils.

Relations with local authorities were the respon-sibility of the District Inspectors, assigned within every division to liaise with each authority, in addition of course to their subject or phase responsibilities. The local authority's own inspectors or advisers were well known to the HMIs assigned to their locality, and in many cases relationships included joint working on courses for teachers and similar initiatives. However, HMIs were moved every few years to prevent any 'cosiness' developing in relations with local authorities. The independence of HMIs, and their ability to be fiercely critical when necessary, was of paramount importance.

The judgements of HMI in the thousands of visits made each year to classrooms in schools and colleges were centrally recorded and analysed, and published in reports both on individual schools and aspects of education nationally, as well as in an annual summary report on the overall state of the national system as it was provided by local authorities. The evidence produced by HMI was always hugely important to ministers and to departmental officials in shaping their policies nationally. HMI specialists were available in most meetings which ministers convened with their senior civil servants, and provided the evidential base of thousands of classroom and school observations from their specialist teams to enhance government decision-making.

The statutory task of HMIs was not to become themselves involved in school improvement. It was primarily to report to the Secretary of State on the state of the nation's education. The massive reports on primary, secondary, early years and teacher education which were produced in the 1970s and 1980s were hugely influential not only in this country but in other major nations throughout the world. Reports such as *A Framework for the School Curriculum* in 1980, *Promoting Curriculum Innovation* in 1982 and *Curriculum Matters* in 1985 formed the basis for government policies on the curriculum. Reports on *The New Teacher in School* in 1982 and *Teaching Quality* in 1983 were to assist government policies in teacher education during that decade.

Improvement in performance at the local level was to be achieved through HMI reports to heads, to governors of schools and ultimately to local authorities whose legal duty it was to provide education fit for the needs of their local population. HMIs were specifically kept from involvement with school improvement, as this was the task of the school, its governors and ultimately the local authority. HMIs were the professional mirror held up to an institution and to a local authority to tell them where there were both strengths and failings, and to report on their performance in published reports and in private discussions with the providers.

No doubt there were weaknesses in the system. During the 1960s, many schools were failing to provide the excellence in standards which successive governments had sought. A dangerous combination emerged of laissez-faire on the part of central government, political correctness in local government and some over-enthusiastic educators in local authorities, colleges and departments of education in universities. These unlikely allies combined to plunge some schools—though by no means all—into experiments with children which were more concerned with politics and social engineering than with achievement outcomes. Some of these experiments were highly successful and indeed inspiring; others were a disastrous abandonment of the core duty of providing each child's entitlement under the law for an appropriate education. In 1967, the Plowden Report, which gave official recognition to what became known as 'progressive education', was enthusiastically accepted by the Wilson government.

Within the inspectorate there were some, though again by no means all, who were enthused by the prevailing Plowden philosophy and who joined in what proved to be the misplaced concept of each child responsible for their own learning. It is important to recognise, however, that at the same time, HMI contributed to the Plowden Inquiry with a huge survey of all primary schools in which they judged only one per cent to be of outstanding quality, with the majority being 'run of the mill' or adequate, and a minority failing badly to provide for the children in their care. These judgements led to the Report's recommendation for educational priority areas (EPAs) to be designated, where children who were most disadvantaged would receive additional funding and resources to raise standards.

The euphoria created by the Plowden Report's philosophy soon began to fade as people realised that, no matter how well the few outstanding schools were able to deal with the child-centred approach, the great majority were unable to cope with such a demanding philosophy, and indeed, near chaos was to be found in many schools. Even in Oxfordshire, an authority much praised by Plowden, I myself visited schools in the early 1970s where children were running aimlessly about in the open-plan areas designed according to the recommended approach, with no structure for the day or teacher control of the environment, and where no visible learning was to be found.

HMIs were not slow to report what was going wrong. I well remember the furore created by damning HMI reports on provision in the Inner London Education Authority and in Haringey, for example. The judgement that such authorities and schools were failing in their duty was loudly criticised by some leading educationalists, as well as, of course, by the providers in those high-spending authorities.

The reforms of teacher education in the 1980s were also HMI-led. The intention of Keith Joseph, who was then Secretary of State, was to roll back the trend to produce teachers who were more informed about educational theory than about the subject they were to teach. Indeed, in some courses the future teacher emerged with no academic discipline other than educational studies, no gift of knowledge or inspirational love of a subject to pass on to their pupils. Circular 3/84 was a landmark in teacher education, requiring as it did that all future teachers should have a grasp of a subject at a level appropriate to higher education, and additionally, that all those who lectured in education should have themselves demonstrated success in their teaching careers.

In 1991, Prime Minister John Major felt deep concern that standards in public services, including education, were not high enough. I was invited to an away-day weekend at Chequers, along with others with experience and expertise in the public sector, to discuss how standards in public service delivery could be raised. My contribution was to be on the topic of inspection as a tool to bear on standards in schools. My advice was that inspection needed to be more frequent, and kept separate from both the providers and the professionals. I asked that a clear definition should be held of an inspector as the friend only of the 'customer', that is the pupil, parent, employer and ultimately also taxpayer. I also argued that inspection should be independent of audit, as audit is a measure of efficiency, while inspection should be a measure of effectiveness.

I marked up the dangers of a local authority inspectorate as too closely involved with the schools they were supposed to judge, and too able, as some cases in the 1960s had demonstrated, to promulgate their own sometimes idiosyncratic ideas about education throughout the schools in their authority. I suggested that the local authority inspectorates should be more nationally accountable, through HMI.

Much of this thinking was accepted by the government, and was incorporated in the Act which was introduced in Parliament the following year. Once the government had decided that all schools should have what used to be called a full inspection every four years, clearly the current establishment of HMI would not serve the purpose. Much larger numbers of people involved in inspections were needed, and the full-time complement of inspectors would have to be supplemented by part-timers. The decision was that the new-style inspection was to be substantially supplied by commercial companies, who charged schools for inspection and who worked to a pattern which was nationally determined. Crucially, when Ofsted was set up, it was as a separate department. No longer were HMI reports to be made to the Secretary of State and published by him or her; Ofsted was now responsible directly for its own published reports.

This system fundamentally changed the role of inspection. From now on, inspectors were not to report to the Secretary of State and stand back from the detail of school improvement; they were the public judges of individual school performance, and the plans the

49

school made for putting right the faults which inspectors had identified. Schools could be put into 'special measures' as a result of the published reports, with huge impact on the local community, as well as on the morale of pupils and staff. In some cases this negative outcome was worthwhile, when the special measures resulted in long-term improvement, but all too often schools have moved in and out of special measures, as the improvements have proved short-term.

Under the Act, local authority inspectorates were effectively disbanded, and many of the inspectors found employment with the companies contracted to what became Ofsted. Since then, local authorities have gradually expanded their developmental capacity through school improvement teams, many of whom perform the job which local advisers and inspectors previously performed. Until last year, when the organisation of Ofsted changed in quite important ways, the day-to- day task of inspection of schools was carried out mainly by part-timers, not necessarily all having been at any time engaged in teaching or possessing any educational qualifications. Because of this, and because the government wished to have a quantifiable assessment of the quality of a school's provision, over the last 15 years the Ofsted inspector has become little more than a clerical officer ticking off pre-determined boxes of what should be judged, rather than a senior professional exercising professional judgement of the quality of pupils' learning. This aspect was far from the structure I or others had envisaged for the new system.

As over the years from 1994 the Ofsted judgements became much more metric and more audit-related, with an emphasis on 'pass' or 'fail' summary judgements, the concept of a 'failing school' was nationally trumpeted as a means to raise standards throughout the system. No doubt the identification of schools where there was substantial evidence of under-performance of pupils was well-intentioned. We were, and alas still are, as a nation, failing to provide adequate educational outcomes for large numbers of our children. The question must be asked, though, as to whether the Ofsted approach has done enough to raise the bar for those most disadvantaged. The answer to that question is sadly that for the lowest achieving schools, and the most disadvantaged children, the gap between their performance and that of the high-achieving schools and pupils has widened over the past decade, not narrowed. At the top 200 schools, 95 per cent of pupils get five or more good GCSEs, while at the bottom, only four per cent achieve this level. Such disparity of opportunity is not acceptable in any civilised and developed society.

Although Ofsted was set up with good intentions and high hopes, we must nevertheless conclude that it has not succeeded in becoming the force for educational achievement that successive governments had hoped. HMI were doing a very different job from that assigned to Ofsted, and had their failings too, no doubt. They did, however, command the respect both of ministers and of the teaching profession—not an inconsiderable achievement! Their removal to Ofsted has left education as the only public service government department with no body of professional advisers on whom ministers can call for advice and action. It is my view that a reform of the system is now urgently needed. Such a reform should restore the provision of high-achieving professionals working within the relevant government department to monitor the system as a whole. Giving them power, on the ministers' behalf, to oversee the school improvement efforts of local authorities and the many schools now outside local authority control, might be a better long-term model to bring about the successful educational provision throughout all schools in our nation that we all so dearly wish to see.

5   Ofsted: Overseeing the Tyranny of Testing

Warwick Mansell*

The most significant speech about Ofsted inspections in recent years was delivered by David Miliband to the North of England education conference in January, 2004. Miliband, who at the time was nearing the end of a two-year stint as Schools Minister, set out the basis on which the current inspection regime is founded. Schools are still living with the consequences. And the education service as a whole is, I would contend, vastly the poorer as a result.

Miliband introduced the concept of 'intelligent accountability', a term coined by the academic Onora O'Neill in calling for the government to be more sophisticated in the way it judged schools and other areas of the public sector. Miliband agreed. Yet his solution was very different from the one envisaged by Lady O'Neill, a cross-bench peer who advocates greater trust of public service professionals. Miliband said it was time for the government to step back. Where previously the Ofsted inspection system had been geared to policing every aspect of a school's performance, including using lengthy lesson observations to judge teaching quality, now it had to become

---

*   Warwick Mansell is writing in his role as an education reporter and author.

more focused. The key, he said, was for inspectors to look at the 'outcomes' achieved by schools for their pupils, rather than worrying too much about the methods they took to bring about any improvements in these end measures. He added that it was necessary to consider whether in-depth inspections of schools of up to a week in length, which had been a feature of the inspection system since Ofsted's introduction in 1992, were the best use of the state's resources. Might it not be better, was the implicit suggestion, to cut the length of them to save money?

Both of these statements dovetailed neatly with two key government priorities at the time. First, they fitted with the seemingly wise mantra of delivering more money to the front-line of public service reform—in this case, the classroom itself—rather than to supporting functions such as the inspectorate. At a time when Ofsted was about to undergo the largest expansion in its remit ever, with its extension to children's social care and adult learning, the logic of this move is clear: the new regime would be cheaper.

Second, and more fundamentally, Miliband's claims matched a drive across the civil service for it to focus not on micro-managing how public sector institutions go about improving their provision, but simply to hold them to account for the results they achieve for those they serve. This also appears sensible. The great danger, many within government now argue, for a public sector which lacks the focus on the bottom line which characterises private firms, is that money is pumped into the system but wasted on bureaucracy, with little end product for the users of public services. As Matthew Taylor, former public services adviser to Tony Blair, wrote recently: 'Poor performance [and] a loss of focus on outcomes are endemic vulnerabilities for big institutions, however laudable a system's objectives and methods.'[1]

In education, Miliband's concerns have been translated into an inspection system which is much more focused on pupils' test and exam results, as the 'outcome' measure for the schooling system, than it was in previous years. And it is my contention that this has been hugely damaging. It is helping to turn education even further towards a bleak and narrow vision that sees its defining purpose as being to maximise the next set of test scores. Yet the assumptions on which this rests are both simplistic and questionable, while the exam results data which now drive most inspections are often unreliable and vulnerable to manipulation.

The first question to consider, in evaluating the current inspection regime, is to what degree pupil test and exam outcomes now influence the verdict which each school receives from inspectors. That is, how much does children's success in the national tests they must sit at seven, 11 and 14, and GCSEs, A-levels and vocational exams, affect their school's Ofsted verdict?

Results have become much more significant after inspections changed in 2005, in line with Miliband's proposals. In the 13 years from the introduction of Ofsted in 1992 to 2005, inspections followed a well-worn pattern. Inspectors spent several days in a school, forming views of its quality by watching teaching, looking at pupils' work, analysing their test and exam results and talking to staff and children, before writing up their judgement. Since 2005, the inspection scenario has changed dramatically. The process now starts with schools providing a pre-inspection report, which consists of their own analysis of their strengths and weaknesses. Inspectors then go into the school and spend a much shorter time than under the old regime—typically, in a secondary school, a day and a half—checking if the school's verdict is correct. Crucially, before having done so, they will have conducted their own desk-based checks on the school's qualities, in which the results of its pupils in national tests—the statutory assessments all children have to sit at age seven, 11 and 14—and exams—mainly GCSEs, A-levels and vocational courses—will have been central. Even after visiting the school, test and exam scores are the inspectors' main measure of its quality.

In early 2006, the Association of School and College Leaders, the secondary heads' union, started reporting that inspectors were arriving at many schools having already made up their minds on what their verdict would be, based solely on the school's test and exam result data. Ofsted, embarrassed that its regime of school visits might be seen as unnecessary, took action. It warned its inspectors in the spring of 2006 that results statistics, while 'informing', should not 'determine' their judgements. This remains its position.

Yet, two years on, the complaints from heads remain. One cheekily wrote: 'This is no way to assess our pupils',[2] and suggested that inspectors should simply short-cut the inspection process by looking at the data and then either writing to schools to tell them that they were outstanding, or starting proceedings to close them down. Another said he would be judged 'totally' by inspectors on the number of his pupils who achieved the central government benchmark for primary schools: the percentage of pupils achieving the target level in national curriculum English, maths and science tests. Are these heads right? Are Ofsted inspections really little more than a check on schools' academic achievements, as measured, also, by league tables?

Thankfully, it is no longer necessary to consider only anecdotal evidence in checking the veracity of these claims. Ofsted itself now provides data on all of its inspection verdicts in recent years. An analysis of these judgements shows just how clear the link between a school's test and exam results and its overall judgement is. Ofsted visited 6,331 primaries in 2006-07, the last academic year for which results are available. Of these, 98 per cent had the same inspection verdict overall as they had for 'achievement and standards'. This latter judgement is based on pupils' test scores, and is only one of six main sub-headings within each inspection. The other sub-headings focus on children's personal development; the quality of teaching; the curriculum; care and guidance offered to pupils; and the strength of the school's leadership. Among secondary schools, the apparent link between exam results and the overall verdict was almost as strong,

57

with 96 per cent gaining the same summing-up judgement as they were awarded on 'achievement and standards'.

Ofsted now uses a four-point judgement scale: outstanding provision is rated 1, and inadequate 4. In not one single school of the 7,612 visited that year did the overall judgement differ by more than a single grade from that given to a school on the basis of its results. Figures for 2005-06, the only other previous year on record since the introduction of the new Ofsted regime, suggest a similar link. Yet the statistics show that there is a far lower association between Ofsted's verdict on other aspects of school life and the overall outcome. For example, only 41 per cent of primary schools received the same overall judgement, in 2006-07, as the inspectors reached on how much pupils enjoyed coming to school.

The emphasis of the inspection system on results statistics stands to be even further accentuated in future, with the promise that schools with good scores might go six years between inspections, while those where exam results are low will be visited every year. Indeed, Ofsted even admits the centrality of test and exam results to its inspectors' overall verdicts on schools. When I put to Ofsted the strikingly high correlation between the judgement reached on test results and the outcome of inspections, the inspectorate replied: 'We would expect these two grades to be the same, or very similar, in the vast majority of inspections. This is because achievement is arguably the most important of all the grades. Other aspects of the report—personal development... leadership and management—all contribute to how well learners achieve.'[3]

But can a valid assessment of an education service be founded almost entirely on pupils' test and exam results? And is the purpose of education simply to maximise children's grades?

In fact, while the current data-driven inspection regime may fit an ideology which says public services are to be defined almost completely in terms of outcomes they achieve for those who use them, and be relatively cheap, it brings with it a host of problems. There are two aspects to this. The first could be characterised as the effect on schools' behaviour of an inspection regime that puts such weight on improving exam scores. It is to accentuate test-orientated teaching, and moves by schools which are understandable, given the pressures on them, and encouraged by the system by which they are judged, to manipulate the results statistics to their advantage.

The introduction of school league tables in the early 1990s under the Conservatives, followed by New Labour's launch of targets for school improvement and test-orientated performance pay for teachers, mean that even without Ofsted in its current form, teachers would be very focused on improving test scores. English pupils face more centrally-monitored tests than their counterparts anywhere else. In most primaries, children encounter a government-designed test at the end of years two, three, four and five, before the major Sats hurdle: the Key Stage 2 tests in English, maths and science. In the four-month run-up to these tests in May, data from the Qualifications and Curriculum Authority reveal that schools spend nearly half the teaching week, on average, on test preparation. In the meantime, non-tested subjects such as history, geography and music receive less curriculum time. Then, in secondary schools, pupils spend most of Year 9 preparing for Key Stage 3 tests in English, maths and science, before embarking on GCSE and A-level courses for which they can now expect final exams almost every term. In the coming two years, new modular GCSE courses which allow re-sits and examining to be staged over the two-year course and yet more tests—'functional skills' exams designed to respond to employers' concerns about school-leavers' mastery of the three Rs—will be introduced. This will mean that many pupils' last five years of secondary school will consist largely of exam preparation.

Does this define a good education? Well, it is fair to say there are many who have doubts, not least the university admissions tutors who are presented with the products of this regime and who have, as a 2005 report by the Nuffield Foundation suggests, grave worries about the benefits of an exam-driven system. The report, based on focus group work with 250 university representatives, said: 'Narrow account-ability based on exam success... needs to be avoided. This leads to spoon-feeding rather than the fostering of independence and critical engagement with subject material.'[4] An inspection system which says, in effect,

that school success depends on pupils' scores throughout their education is only reinforcing this trend.

The government argues throughout, in defending
its system of school accountability of which inspections
are a key strand, that it does not encourage professionals to focus only on a narrow approach to test
success. But this misses the point that the assumptions
on which the regime is based, and the consequences for
those failing to improve the test scores, push many
teachers towards doing so.

The second problematic aspect of the modern
inspection regime is the question of whether the results
that the tests and exams generate provide useful and
reliable information about the quality of education
which they are meant to assess. It is not always clear
that good test results equal good teaching. There is, in
fact, copious evidence that test scores can be boosted
by short-term test preparation or cramming—often
repetitive practice of questions similar to those which
are likely to appear in the forthcoming test—which
does little for students' long-term understanding or
engagement with the subject. Does this constitute good
teaching, as Ofsted's system would suggest it does, so
long as good results are generated by it?

Ironically, some of the best evidence suggesting that
the above question could be answered in the negative
comes from Ofsted itself, in annual reports published
before the introduction of the latest inspection regime.
David Bell's chief inspector's report for 2004-05 said, of
Key Stage 3 English, for example: 'In many schools, too
much time is devoted to test revision, with not enough

regard to how pupils' skills could be developed in more meaningful ways.'[5] For maths, Ofsted concluded for the same year: 'National test results continue to improve but this is as much due to better test technique as it is to a rise in standards of mathematical understanding.' In science, a report for the Wellcome Trust this year, based on a survey of 600 teachers and focus group interviews with 74 of them, found that pupils were being turned off science by the two terms of revision they received in the run-up to the Key Stage 2 tests pupils take at 11.[6] Yet, said focus group members 'test preparation in its current form contributed little to pupils' understanding', while most teachers did not trust the test results as verdicts on their pupils' underlying abilities, partly because of the hot-housing needed to boost the scores.

The statistical formulae on which the Ofsted inspection framework sits can also be manipulated, so that the outcome may say more about a school's ability to play the results 'game' than about the underlying quality of the service it provides for pupils.

Two examples best illustrate this. First, many schools have had to become adept at focusing on a narrow band of pupils, known widely as 'borderliners', who have the most potential to improve an institution's headline statistics. In primary schools, this is the group of children who are identified as being on the cusp of achieving the government benchmark of level four in the Key Stage 2 tests. In secondaries, those at risk of narrowly missing a level five in the Key Stage 3 tests, or a C grade at GCSE, are also the focus.

Routinely, now, schools give these pupils extra attention in terms of after-school revision classes and
mentoring by older pupils and/or their teachers.

Second, secondary schools can choose to push their
pupils towards GCSE-equivalent courses which are
given high weighting in the formulae, such as
vocational exams which are counted as 'worth' four
GCSEs despite being widely seen as a soft option for
teenagers. Thus the good results generated by the
school say more about the assumptions on which the
statistical formulae rest than about underlying teaching
quality.

Parents' views are also marginalised by a system
which now rests so much on statistical representations
of what constitutes a good school. Under the old
arrangements, schools had to send out a parental
questionnaire in advance of the inspection. Inspectors
then collated the findings, published them in their
report and, crucially, also explained their position
when parents' views differed from those of the inspection team. In the current Ofsted system, although the
parental questionnaires are still sent out, inspectors
have little time to consider the responses in detail.
They are not written up for the report, and no
justification is given when the inspection judgement
differs from parents' views.

In fact, there is little space for this in the new
reports, which offer much sparser information on
school quality than was possible before 2005. In my
recent book on the test regime, *Education by Numbers*, I
compared two Ofsted secondary school reports from

2002, under the old regime, with two from 2006, under the new. The old reports weigh in at 50 and 61 pages respectively, against five pages each for their 2006 counterparts. In both 2006 reports, almost the entire summary on the school's effectiveness—from the quality of the school's curriculum to the pastoral care it provides—relates to test data. What is left unmeasured in the results statistics on which the new system rests? Well, extra-curricular activities and, in primary schools, any subjects which are not English, maths and science are all marginalised.

If one accepts Ofsted's justification of the new regime, however, this is not so. For all aspects of school life, it argues, contribute to pupils' (test and exam) achievements. They are thus, indirectly, captured through test data, since a pupil given a rounded educational experience and who is enjoying his or her school life is more likely to succeed. This might sound a persuasive argument in theory. But the idea that every aspect of school life can be captured and measured through the statistical formulae of exam success, is, I would submit, simplistic and naïve. Neither would common sense suggest that every life-enriching experience a pupil has at school will have an immediate pay-off in terms of exam success.

Yet schools are being judged in this way. One primary head teacher, whose school failed its inspection in late 2005, put it this way: 'In every section of the inspection report we were criticised for the same thing: standards (i.e. test scores). In "teaching and learning" the reason we got a 4 (the lowest category) was because standards were not good enough... The care and support we gave children was down because our academic support (as measured by test scores) was "inadequate". And my "leadership and management" was down because the statistics were inadequate. In every section, we were damned because of poor test results.'

In fact, Ofsted's argument fits the theoretical rationale which was used to justify the current structure of the inspection regime, rather than being based on the reality on the ground. The assumption is that all aspects of education contribute directly to immediate exam success, and that pupil outcomes matter more than the means used to achieve them. Yet I would argue that the means by which students achieve good grades are hugely important. A pupil who has managed to gain a particular level in a test at age 11 at the cost of a narrowed curriculum and months of repetitive question practice has not received an educational experience I would want for my children, if I were a parent.

Inputs, in terms of the quality of teaching as distinct from the 'outcomes' it generates for pupils, are important in this context. Education, I would contend, has value in itself, not just in terms of the immediate exam success it generates for pupils. Any inspection system, then, has to find a way of assessing the quality of teaching not simply through outcome statistics. An obvious way to do this would be to return to the old system of much more direct observation of lessons. Test results can only ever be a proxy for good teaching.

And they are a limited one, because they test only a proportion of the curriculum. For example, pupils' speaking skills are not assessed in English exams until 16, while in science experimental work is not assessed in any government test until GCSE.

There is one final objection to the argument that Ofsted inspectors are right to base their verdicts to such a large extent on schools' exam results. Although there might seem to be some logic in the notion that public services should be judged on their ability to 'deliver' better outcomes for those who use them, the generation of good exam results for pupils differs from other measures of public sector success. For, unlike, say, success rates of a surgeon on the operating table or the ability of companies to get their trains to run on time, the consumers themselves have a key role to play in the generation of good school results. Indeed, exams were originally conceived wholly as a way of assessing the qualities of the pupil, rather than his or her school. Pupil motivation and effort, then, have always been thought to be a key element in securing good marks.

In trying to make them, now, much more of a verdict on the quality of those educating the child, inspectors are underlining the view that improving test and exam scores almost have to be achieved for pupils come what may. In this way, student agency is down-graded: they become a much more passive recipient of education, and are sent the message that their teacher must, essentially, achieve the results for them. This is not just a theoretical argument. The best evidence of how it is happening in reality comes with GCSE coursework, for which many teachers now confess to routinely telling pupils what to write, since they cannot afford for them to fail to achieve the grades on which a school's future may hinge.

A quotation from an academic in the Nuffield Foundation report also reflects the knock-on effect of this among undergraduates: 'I don't like the "empty file pad syndrome", when students arrive at a seminar with an empty pad, waiting for solutions simply to be communicated to them. The attitude is often "what do I need to know in order to be able to do the examination?" There's a search for people who break out of that mould.' Ofsted inspections are, I believe, now the most influential factor in encouraging teaching to the test and reduction of education to exam preparation.

When league tables were introduced, schools could at least take the view that they would not become 'exams factories' focusing relentlessly on test success. If results were slightly lower in consequence, at least parents could be the judge of whether or not the trade-off was a price worth paying. Now, under the new Ofsted inspection regime, schools are facing a choice of going down the better-grades-at-all-cost route, or potentially being failed by inspectors impatient with any action which does not maximise pupil achievement, as measured by its results formulae. I believe that this is pernicious, at worst leaving Ofsted's role as an enforcer of the political agenda of ministers to raise test scores, almost come what may. For New Labour's system of targets has ensured that statistical indicators of pupils' test success are how the politicians are judged.

At the very least, this new regime should not be accepted without a detailed and public debate about whether the purpose of education is solely, as the modern inspection framework clearly implies, to improve exam grades, or whether the public has a right to expect something more from it.

6

The Experience of an 'Outstanding Provider'

Bavaani Nanthabalan[*]

The strengths of the current section 5 inspection system

During my teaching career, I have witnessed three Ofsted inspections. As well as a section 5 inspection at Torriano Junior School in North London in 2005, I have experienced two section 10 inspections; one in 1996 and one in 2001. In both those inspections I was observed as a class teacher and as a subject leader and deputy head.

The current section 5 Ofsted inspection process is, in my view, a swift, sharp and responsive model. For our school, it was an intense process but the views expressed by my leadership team, staff and children, have been very positive. The inspection provided an accurate snapshot of the school on our journey of school improvement. We found it to be a positive experience because it was a validation of where we were and where we thought that we needed to go.

From our perspective at Torriano Junior School there are four key factors under section 5 that are an improvement to the previous system of Ofsted inspection.

Firstly, the short notice meant that we were being judged on our *actual* practice, standards and expect-

---

[*] Bavaani Nanthabalan is writing in her role as a head teacher.

ations of pupils. The previous section 10 inspection, by comparison, had become burdensome as schools over-prepared for inspection and lost their way. In short, under the former system, inspection was treated as the day of judgement. Much of the three months prior to Ofsted's arrival was spent preparing for the perfect inspection through meticulous planning of lessons, displays and paperwork from every subject co-ordinator, for the inspectors' perusal. Good schools already had exemplary standards and systems in place to raise their pupil achievement but there were schools that were able to present themselves in a positive light because of the long notice given. The lead-up to an inspection was spent preparing the school environment and the week's lessons for external observation. Within the new regime, this is no longer the case. Our school improvement plan, for example, was not written with Ofsted in mind, but rather driven by our school's needs.

Secondly, the focus within the section 5 regime on school self-evaluation is absolutely right. When we received 'the call' from Ofsted, informing us of the inspection date, there was nervousness in the school, but that is natural when there is any form of scrutiny. However, as a school we were confident, because my governors, staff and I were running the school to meet children's needs. Under the section 10 model, by contrast, schools were producing documentation that was not needed for internal use. In my experience, the self-evaluation form (SEF), although not statutory, has been highly beneficial and was to be a key document in the section 5 inspection. As a new head in a 'coasting' school, I used the SEF as a tool for assessing standards and managing progress i.e. to assess the school's strengths and weaknesses, raise expectations and address complacence. It proved an important vehicle of change for the school because it helped develop an urgency in our staff to set higher expectations for themselves and our pupils.

Having set the tone as a school, I have found that there is little need to be obsessive with the SEF, but to remain focused on self-evaluation based on a wider range of evidence.

Thirdly, the ethos of the section 5 inspection was very different to previous section 10 inspections. We felt that we were, in effect, in a dialogue with the inspection team for two days, and that the inspection was done *with* us and not *to* us. We respected the process: we felt that the inspectors were credible and therefore their findings contributed to our school self-improvement plan. We certainly felt that we were being listened to. For example, we were able to talk about transition from Year 2 to Year 3 and explain the evidence we had collated to track the progress of one cohort of children from entry at Year 3 to Year 5. It enabled us to show progress despite a dip in standards at Year 3 in comparison to the children's attainment at Year 2. The lead inspector also took time to read the head teacher's reports to the governing body, which conveyed the school's performance according to the Every Child Matters outcomes.

Finally the section 5 inspection raised expectations of leadership at all levels—for subject leaders, the senior leadership team and governors. The evidence was strongly focused on pupil assessment data which meant that the emphasis was very much on academic outcomes. This was very welcome but the onus was on us to produce the proof; we had to raise our game. We had to be conversant with the PANDA (performance and assessment reports, now reborn as 'Raiseonline') and our school data, in order to interpret the evidence and use it to support our own judgements of pupil progress in school.

The inspectors were knowledgeable and precise. Senior leaders were expected to know the quality of teaching and learning across the school and it felt as though the inspectors really did test this aspect to see if it matched our assessment. It supported our move towards senior leadership team responsibility for monitoring standards, rather than making it exclusive to the head and deputy head.

The weaknesses in the current inspection system

Data drives the inspection. Although the logic is understandable, there are drawbacks. Unlike the section 10 regime, the new inspection system relies largely on value-added performance. Inspectors based their judgements on the PANDA and despite the fact that we were able to show year-on-year improvement of one cohort, and a total of five out of seven lessons observed were graded by the inspectors as 'outstanding', the 'teaching and learning' was graded good but not outstanding. Similarly, 'standards and achievement' were also graded only good. It seemed there was a formula by which the inspectors determined their grades and our inspector seemed reluctant to deviate from this.

Experienced and confident inspection teams can get it right, but a narrow focus on data, to the exclusion of more comprehensive evidence gathered in inspection, can detract from children's wider achievement and attitudes. There can also be inconsistency between inspection teams. Inspectors inexperienced in inner London settings, for example, may be easily impressed by ethnic minority achievement if expectations are low, particularly as contextualised value-added data compares, for example, Bangladeshi children against the achievement of other Bangladeshi children. Furthermore, the data that inspectors look at relates solely to literacy and numeracy, to the exclusion of learning in the other subjects. Children's ability to contribute to a socially cohesive society is hugely important and how a school prepares its pupils for life can be missed altogether. There was little time for the inspectors to inspect the five outcomes of Every Child Matters, as well as the foundation subjects. In fact, the foundation subjects seem to have lost their status in inspectors' minds.

Torriano is a junior school and for us a smooth transition (from the infants) is a big issue. We take children from an infant school and their results at Key Stage 1 appear, at times, inflated. Our school then has the task of sustaining some very high average point scores which may not be an accurate assessment of children's achievement. This can de-motivate children and skew the curriculum. True, there are differences in Key Stage 1 and Key Stage 2 testing; but the 'value-added' progress by our school is based on the infant school's performance. More thought could be put into the way that the two school inspections are timed and carried out to pick up on these issues of transition and progression.

Parents' views are no longer gathered as well as they were in the section 10 inspection. In the previous system, parents had an opportunity to have a free and frank meeting with the inspection team. Relying on questionnaires, as is now necessary, is not sufficient considering that we have parents who would be averse to completing a piece of paper which is not the ideal means of communication for them. This may not be true of schools in areas that have parents who are more literate in the English language. I know of a school in our locality which resorted to going from door-to-door in order to get parents to complete the survey. Ethnic minority parents would appreciate the opportunity to meet with inspectors and express their views face to face. It is a valuable way of recognising their contribution to the process. Ethnic minority parents would also be able to inform inspectors on whether the school is as inclusive as it states in the SEF, particularly as the expectation is that Every Child Matters. It is not merely a question of meeting the needs of children new to English, but of raising their achievement; and that can only happen with parental involvement. It would be important to evaluate how successful they perceive the school's approach succeeds to this to be. I am also certain that there are other vulnerable social groups of parents (e.g. white working-class parents) who would appreciate a meeting with inspectors. What they say may work for or against a school; whether positive or negative for the school, it would make the Ofsted inspection process a more inclusive one.

Finally, I asked my pupils what their suggestion for an improvement to the inspection process would be: they said that there should be no notice given to schools. Inspectors should come in and see us as we are!

7

Hanging by a Hair: Ofsted's Damoclesian Sword

Graham Lester George[*]

All parents worry about giving their children the best start in life. We do our best to place them in the best school available; one which we hope will equip them with the formal knowledge they need for their careers, as well as a broad understanding of the world and themselves which will help them to be good human beings.

In recent years league tables and Ofsted reports have become the benchmarks by which parents choose the best available schools. As children approach the age to go from nursery to primary or from primary to secondary school, anxious parents scan websites and newspapers to see which schools are at the top of their game. Then we enter the nerve-wracking application process. 'What if we put Brightmore School down as our first choice and are refused, will Cleverly City Academy also turn us down because they were second choice? If that happens, then... that only leaves Dunstone Comp where the best GCSE marks were in Car Maintenance and Hairdressing.'

But how can we be sure that, armed with these tables and reports, we are making a truly informed choice? When our middle son went up to Year 4 at his

---

[*] Graham Lester George is writing as a parent.

inner-city primary school, our youngest son came up from the nursery to begin Year 1. And in that year the much liked and admired head teacher announced his early retirement. He was 'old school'. He had invested his life in doing his best for the children in his charge, and to good effect. A constant presence in the corridors and playground, he was always approachable by parents and knew all 350 plus pupils by name. None of the parents I knew doubted his commitment and dedication. But he had had enough. The political diktats from the then DfES and the pressures from the local education authority (LEA) and Ofsted had made him see that he could no longer employ his experience and skill as he saw fit as an educator of young minds.

When the new head took control the following year it soon became clear that she had a very different style. Having seen the political writing on the educational wall, she was a convert; whether through conviction or expediency is hard to say. But the atmosphere in the school changed radically. The staff was split into two conflicting camps; several teachers and teaching assistants resigned within the year, and several of us parents, including the chair of governors, decided to move our children to other schools.

But where to? We consulted Ofsted reports and league tables, and we also asked around, questioning parents about their children's schools. One school seemed to shine out among the rest. Not only had its last Ofsted report been well above average, but parents positively glowed with praise for the head's nurturing and enlightened approach to their children's education; an important part of which was a healthy emphasis on the arts and humanities. We also learned that not only was the head highly regarded by his peers but also by the LEA, to the extent that they had asked him to take on an additional school which was 'failing'. Flattering as this must have been, he had apparently refused.

In order to judge the man for ourselves, we made an appointment to meet him. We liked him. We liked his ethos and his school very much. And so we applied for a place only to be turned down by the LEA on the grounds that we were out of the area and the school was over-subscribed. Our appeal was also turned down and so our sons had to remain for the time being at their original school.

The following year, when our elder son went up to secondary school, our youngest was at last granted a place in Year 3 of our preferred school. He soon settled in and both he and we were happy—for a year and a half. Then 'An Inspector Called'.

Well, several Ofsted inspectors. Within two days the school was declared to be failing and put into special measures. The effect was so sudden and so devastating that one member of staff likened it to 'a nuclear wind blasting through the school'. What we saw as parents were our children's hitherto highly competent and confident teachers now filled with self-doubt, their head with 30 years of dedicated service defamed, and our happy and well functioning school despoiled of its reputation and stigmatised. Overnight.

The head left in a state of shock, his credibility destroyed and his lifelong career in education ruined. Several other members of staff took sick-leave and some subsequently resigned. All this on the basis of a two-day inspection.

How could we have got it so wrong: we parents, many of whom were well-educated, well-informed professional people who believed in the school, its standards and ethos? How had the head, staff and children conspired to hide such gross mismanagement and incompetence from us?

Well of course they hadn't. Nothing had fundamentally changed since the previous inspection. Or had it? Well yes it had. The head had since become a vociferous critic, on both local and national platforms, of the government's target-led approach to education and our LEA's implementation of it. He among others had been highlighting how the pressure on every school (be it leafy suburban or deprived inner-city) to deliver uniformly good Sats results was having an adverse effect on education. How this, combined with an aggressive and punitive inspection regime, was frightening school heads and their staff into becoming cheats, lest they fail to deliver (if you find these assertions less than credible, then I suggest you tap 'Sats' + 'cheating' into a search engine and see what comes up). Needless to say, our head did not countenance cheating or 'teaching to the test' in his own school.

In the days following the Ofsted visit, we parents were to be found huddled in groups in the playground, shell-shocked and confused. A few weaker vessels, who had previously been enthusiastic supporters of the school, now began to doubt their own instincts and experience. But for the majority, confusion turned to anger. The consensus was that there was something very worrying going on, and we were not prepared to accept Ofsted's condemnation at face-value.

I as one of a number of parents who formed the nucleus of what became the Parents' Action Group, drafted the following letter to Ofsted.

Dear Sirs,

OFSTED REPORT ********* PRIMARY SCHOOL

We the undersigned parents of children at ********* Primary School, would like to register our strong dissatisfaction with the conclusions of the inspection report dated 14-15th February 2006. The report's almost unremittingly harsh and damning conclusions and its consequent opinion that the school requires 'special measures' bear little or no relation to ours and our children's experience of the school, its staff and the excellent education and care which we believe they have been providing.

Reading through the report, one is left with the impression that the inspectors approached this school with a blinkered predisposition to find fault, based on narrow and overly prescriptive criteria which do not allow for a holistic view of the school's achievements.

It is our strong belief that the purpose of education is to make children *fit for life*, contrary to the present government's narrower ambition to make children *fit for work.* We observe that the hitherto prevailing ethos of ********** Primary has inculcated a broad love of learning in our children, and a growing ability to analyse and question the world around them. This is evident in their daily enthusiasm to attend school and participate in what it has to offer them. This in stark contrast to the experience of a significant number of parents who chose to move their children from another local school, ********* Primary, which despite a glowing Ofsted report was, in their estimation, failing their children.

Such experiences lead us to question the assessment and reporting methods employed by Ofsted, and its ability to give an accurate and fair picture of a school. There was minimal consultation with us as parents, and a two day snapshot based on overly prescriptive and narrow criteria is not, in our opinion, a sound basis on which to condemn, or indeed praise a school.

We therefore demand that a consultation meeting be convened between the parents, school staff, Ofsted and the LEA, and also that the inspectors' report and methods be thoroughly and independently reviewed.

In conclusion we would like to put on record how much we appreciated the energy, vision and enthusiasm of ****** ********, the excellent former head teacher, and deplore the fact that he felt obliged to resign as a consequence of this Ofsted report.

Yours faithfully,

    Parents' Action Group

Within just a few days it had been signed by 210 parents; by far the majority of parents who were to be found in the playground during that period.

By this time the local press, radio and TV were showing interest, and as spokesperson I was interviewed on a local breakfast show. The local BBC TV news filmed me delivering the petition to Ofsted. Mick Brookes, the general secretary of the National Association of Head Teachers (NAHT) who had by now taken up the cudgels on behalf of our former head, stated on the BBC's *Politics Show* that the NAHT were going to support the sacked head in an action against Ofsted for defamation. *Guardian Education* then picked up the story and splashed it on the front page. Although curiously there were no direct quotes from our former head.

The Parents' Action Group received a reply from Ofsted stating that they would treat our letter as an official complaint, promising to carry out an internal review of the inspection. And so we waited patiently, but not very optimistically, for the outcome.

I called the *Guardian* journalist to update him, and asked him why there had been no quotes in his piece from our former head. He confided that the LEA had offered the head a generous severance package, but strictly on condition that he did not speak to the press. He'd been gagged. One can't blame our former head; this man had laid down his career on our behalf and we should not be expecting him to starve on our behalf as well. But it leaves one with the nagging question:

what was the LEA so afraid of that they had offered money for his silence?

In due course, Ofsted wrote to us again setting out their response to our complaint. Unlike the police, the financial services industry, the utilities companies etc., Ofsted does not have an independent complaints procedure. Our complaint was dealt with by one of their own. They did not re-interview any of the staff or the former head of the school, but based their assessment merely on the report itself. And so we were not greatly surprised to read against each of our points: 'This aspect of your complaint is not upheld.'

In the meantime another head teacher had been brought out of retirement to run the school until a permanent appointment could be made. On the face of it, she had all the right credentials: an OBE for services to education, and a husband who had been an Ofsted inspector.

More than two years after Ofsted and under the direction of new and energetic joint heads, the school is out of special measures, but with a large budget deficit. Our youngest son, now coming to the end of his primary education, has recently taken his Key Stage 2 Sats following an intensive ten-week period of core curriculum revision. Which, although one of the abler children, he described as very stressful. In fact he lost several days to 'stomach-ache' over that period, and he was not the only child to go down with stress-related ailments. But the school has been pulled back into line, and Sats stress among eleven-year-olds has been restored. Hurrah!

Having experienced Ofsted as a parent, I am left with the strong opinion that far from being a force for good, it is an extremely corrosive one. It seems that every school in England has a Damoclesian sword hanging over it. Too many good heads and teachers exist in a climate of fear where their careers and reputations can be destroyed in the space of a two-day visit from Ofsted.

It is my observation that education has become corrupted by political pressure. Sats are not raising standards in schools, they are forcing normally honourable and dedicated teachers to cheat the system: opening Sats papers in advance so that they can 'teach to the test'; posting up 'helpful' material for children to 'discover' during the tests; testing children in the morning and getting them to re-sit in the afternoon with corrected answers pencilled in. Because woe betide any school (regardless of whether it's in a deprived inner city or a well-heeled leafy suburb) which fails to deliver uniformly high test results.

I know many teachers personally (my daughter teaches English in a Birmingham comprehensive), and I've spoken to many more. And they tell me that, in reality, Sats are often meaningless. Government ministers tell us they are raising standards in education. So why are an increasing number of secondary schools now testing their intakes of Year 7s? Could it be that they know the results of Key Stage 2 Sats are too often works of fiction?

8 We Need an Inspection Process — But Not This One

Mick Brookes[*]

This provocative title has two important elements: first of all 'We need an inspection system'. It is fundamentally important to emphasise from the outset, that the NAHT is not an advocate of anarchy. We recognise the need for public accountability and also would welcome observations that may help schools to progress. We also recognise that that accountability must come from an external body. However, the second part of the title is '...but not this one'. There is mounting evidence, both anecdotal and empirical, that the culture and operation of the existing Ofsted system is outmoded, insensitive and has quality assurance difficulties.

On the empirical level, research commissioned by the NAHT and carried out by the University of Central Lancaster has produced interim findings that reinforce the anecdotal evidence collected by our own inspections section. The report, which was published in May 2008, arrived at four main conclusions:

- Inspection outcomes give authority to leadership teams in cases where the findings of the inspection

---

[*] Mick Brookes is writing in his role as General Secretary of the National Association of Head Teachers.

propel the direction of travel defined by school self-evaluation

- The quality of the inspection teams is variable
- The reliance on external data is too heavy
- Ofsted inspections contribute to poor retention and recruitment of school leaders

The first observation is positive, and emphasises the effect that a good inspection system can have in supporting the leadership team in its analysis and development of quality assuring systems and structures. One example where this would be valuable is the newly appointed head teacher who comes into a difficult situation and has opposition to change and development. The authority given by an independent power can be a useful tool in persuading possibly reluctant governors and staff to embrace development.

The comment below, from a head teacher, illustrates this:

> As a new head teacher it [the inspection] pulled the staff together behind me and we have become a very tight team.

However the positive feedback about inspection is noticeably limited: significantly, only one of the four main conclusions from the research is positive. The majority feeling about the inspection process was that it either made no difference or that it was unhelpful.

The quality of the Ofsted inspection teams is another grave concern amongst head teachers, as the comment below illustrates:

> I have had one good experience of an Ofsted [inspection] under the new system but the teams from each of my five inspections at different schools have been so very different and unpredictable—and judgements so varied—that I am unable to say helpful or unhelpful until after the event! And I am the same me!

However, whilst there is much dissatisfaction amongst head teachers, the NAHT has had many contacts from colleagues who have had a difficult time with inspection, but are so traumatised by the experience that they simply want to forget it, and hence don't complain to Ofsted—only to us:

> The lead inspector was insensitive and the report was very poor. I should have complained at the time but felt 'shell-shocked'.

Table 8.1 (p. 88) shows that, worryingly, more than two-thirds of the respondents surveyed report that there is a negative effect on staff morale and energy after the inspection. This is particularly true for the head teacher, one of whom described the experience as 'having the stuffing knocked out of her'. Worse still, many—effective—heads feel compelled to resign because of Ofsted inspections:

> As a direct result of being placed into 'notice to improve' I resigned with effect from the end of the school year. This was something that I was thinking about but the process of the inspection was so bad and its value so poor that if that is the best we can do for the type of pupils in my school then heaven help us!

Table 8. 1
The impact of inspections on schools

	Base	Very helpful	Helpful	No difference	Unhelpful	Very unhelpful
Base	2,789	139 5.0%	541 19.4%	1,034 37.1%	689 24.7%	393 14.1%
Learning of the pupils	462	12 2.6%	124 26.8%	256 55.4%	59 12.8%	13 2.8%
Behaviour of the pupils	461	5 1.1%	37 8.0%	361 78.3%	42 9.1%	16 3.5%
Wellbeing of the staff generally	467	6 1.3%	44 9.4%	79 16.9%	225 48.2%	114 24.4%
Staff morale and energy after the inspection	470	17 3.6%	68 14.5%	62 13.2%	163 34.7%	164 34.9%
The external image of the school	466	62 13.3%	138 29.6%	121 26.0%	97 20.8%	48 10.3%
The school's image of itself	463	37 8.0%	130 28.1%	155 33.5%	103 22.2%	38 8.2%

This brings us on to the reliance on test data. The weight given to statistics is something which is also considered to be a problem despite the fact that we have been assured by Her Majesty's Chief Inspector that external data (in the form of contextual value-added scores) are 'an indicator not a determinant' of inspection outcomes. As can be seen from Table 8.2 (p. 89), an overwhelming number of respondents (88.3 per cent) think that there is too strong an emphasis on external data. Research by Warwick Mansell suggests that 98 per cent of inspection outcomes reflect the judgement on standards as represented by contextual valued-added (CVA) data.[1] As such, there is a strong feeling that those areas not captured by CVA data are not taken into account, when schools are being judged by Ofsted.

One typical comment is that 'although we do many fantastic things with the children in this school, the inspectors either weren't interested or didn't have the time to see them'.

Table 8.2
The use of exam/test data in inspection

Base	470
In your view is the degree of influence on inspection outcomes exerted by statutory testing data?	
Not strong enough	2
About right	53
Too strong	415

The combination of an emphasis on test and exam data, and responsibility for the school management, have led to great pressure for head teachers to sustain good test results. This is illustrated by the following head teacher's comment:

> I am acutely aware that one or two years of dipping Sats results leave a head teacher in an extremely vulnerable position.

Within the current Ofsted regime, our research has found that generally school leaders feel very vulnerable. The NAHT and the National College of School Leadership have identified this vulnerability as contributing to the negative effect on the recruitment and retention of school leaders. In other words, Ofsted inspection is arguably a key contributor to the serious recruitment and retention issue of head teachers in this country. For example, one deputy head, when asked when he was going to apply for a headship, replied: 'I don't think I will, because that will mean I have to go through ten Ofsteds, and I don't want to do that.'

The research is overwhelming in this aspect, with almost nine out of ten respondents citing this negative effect.

Our research shows that, in particular, many deputy heads do not choose to go on to headships, because of the onus upon them of Ofsted inspection. The following comments reflect this scenario:

> I know that this is one of the reasons that my deputy will not and will never apply for headship.

> I won't be applying for headship even though I worked for and gained PQH [Professional Qualification for Headship] only two years ago. I just feel that in my position of Vice Principal too much is expected of me and it is not possible to carry out all the duties demanded.

> Differential in pay between deputy and head not significant enough to warrant such an increase in publicly viewed level of responsibility.

The supply of suitably qualified and enthusiastic head teachers is fundamentally important. The quality of education depends on good leadership. This issue has to be addressed with far greater determination than is currently being shown.

Statistics from Education Data Surveys reveals the impact that inspection has had on head teachers:[2]

- There are no long lists for headships with fewer than three per post in primary and special schools, but a slightly improving picture in the secondary sector

- Re-advertising is at an all-time high with almost half of all headship posts having to be re-advertised in some areas even outside London

The following comments were recorded in the survey about job security for head teachers:

- 'The process made me want to leave education altogether.'

- 'I think all head teachers feel as if they are living from one inspection to the next, and are very vulnerable.'

- 'I have lost all drive and enthusiasm for teaching and leadership after 34 years of teaching including the leadership of a successful school for 13 years.'

- 'I feel very vulnerable. My governors do their best to support me but at times it's a very lonely job. I feel the weight of responsibility for inspection now rests very squarely on the shoulders of the HT [head teacher].'

- 'I am still a good, effective HT, but I feel no sense of security in this post. A local, well-respected HT disappeared overnight after an unsatisfactory inspection. What message does that send to the rest of us?'

- 'In my LA [local authority] the pattern seems to be: fail an inspection and you are asked to resign. At a meeting with the Head of CfBT [the education trust] in my LA I was asked to resign because it is the policy of the members of the Council to ask for this through CfBT—I do wonder if it is legal but of course all the meetings are private and off the record.'

This final comment is one of the most worrying.

- I am in the process of applying to be a head teacher. I will not do this in a school with high mobility, high EAL [English as an additional language], high FSM [free school meals], high SEN [special educational needs] ... as these factors are not really taken into account by the inspection process.

It is the schools with high levels of pupil mobility, English as an additional language, deprivation as measured by whether they are entitled to free school meals and special educational needs that are the schools which are most in need of dynamic, positive leadership. They are also the same schools that are ritually humiliated by the publication of league tables and stand the least chance of a successful inspection based wholly or mainly on exam and test performance.

There is an inversion of social justice here. It is the staff of the schools in those areas with hard-to-teach children and hard-to-reach parents that have the greatest challenge—yet the least reward. Admitting a child with special educational needs is a certain way to reduce Sats scores, and reduced Sats scores result in an unfavourable inspection outcome as surely as night follows day. This is clearly wrong.

A new constructive, rather than destructive, vision of inspection

So if the current system needs to change, what should a new system look like in order to keep the shibboleth of public accountability?

A new system must be built on a different set of values. The current Ofsted inspection regime assumes that the school workforce is inherently lazy and is only motivated by fear of reprisal. It is also built on a foundation of low trust which demands copious amounts of evidence and compliance. If we start from a different place, the outcomes will also be different. A simple truth to begin with is that the vast majority of the school workforce joins the profession in order to make positive differences to children's lives. They need to be supported in this ambition, not castigated. Therefore, a new system should look to find success and address problems in a constructive dialogue with the school. Sanctions should apply only where it is patently obvious that no effort has been taken to address difficult issues.

This can be expressed professionally as:
The school has …
The school needs to …

This pragmatic statement of outcomes removes the 'demonisation' of schools when they are categorised as needing 'special measures' or being 'hard to shift' or requiring 'notice to improve'.

Less reliance on test and exam data

External data can be very useful as long as it informs rather than *determines* inspection outcomes. The fact that it is impossible, on the one extreme, to have a value-added score of anything but satisfactory if you are a grammar school with a high performing intake of Year 7 children is clearly nonsense. At the other extreme it is clearly wrong to penalise a school with high numbers of children with learning difficulties because they are not making the required two levels progress.

Whole school inspection

The whole context of the school should be sampled for inspection. Schools must be given credit for excellence in the arts or sport or science or they will simply stop doing them. If there are such high stakes around the assessment of a narrow range of subjects, the effect will be that the curriculum will be narrowed, thereby narrowing the educational experience of the children.

Inspection timing which doesn't catch schools out

The requirement for re-inspection should be agreed as part of the immediate inspection outcome. The school will set a date for its next inspection at an interval that is appropriate and at a time that is good for the school. This will not be during examination weeks or at the beginning or end of terms when the school will not necessarily be seen in normal working mode.

There must be sensitivity around matters that affect the timing and deferring of inspection. The current insensitivity around traumatic incidents and the refusal to defer are indefensible. Incidents, such as when a head teacher's mother died and the inspection was not allowed to be deferred, are inhumane and not worthy of any professional body.

Higher quality inspection teams

The current teams of inspectors should be disbanded and a professional cadre of HMI should be set up on a regional basis to address the issues of quality assurance. Every inspection must be quality assured.

Finally, inspection should be an experience that is welcomed by schools, although we recognise that there will be a level of anxiety that goes with a robust system. We need to have a system that promotes professional integrity and encourages an atmosphere of openness and trust. Ofsted clearly has a long way to go.

9   What Does Ofsted Inspect? A Steiner Waldorf Perspective

Kevin Avison[*]

The story goes that the day after Prime Minister James Callaghan's famous speech at Ruskin College, on the need to radically raise educational standards, the Cabinet Secretary was ordered to attend Her Majesty's Chief Inspector for a firm dressing down: 'How dare the Prime Minister make a speech about education without consulting me!' That may be apocryphal, but whether fact or fiction, it makes a telling point of contrast: HMI then, Ofsted now. And the journey in between has been immense. While a more recent myth states that schools (and presumably teachers) were failing children until first the National Curriculum and, subsequently, New Labour reforms came along, the narrative lacks any clear chart of progress or formal map to establish when or whether the travellers might have arrived—anywhere, let alone anywhere *better*. Small wonder fierce battles are fought over whether 'standards' are declining or not. What is clear is that Callaghan's speech came to be the first wash of an eventual tidal wave that has swept aside much of what that Prime Minister would have taken for granted in education. Old vagaries were replaced by a profound

---

[*]   Kevin Avison is writing in his role as an executive officer to the Steiner Waldorf Schools Fellowship.

centralisation of education policy and the 'success' or otherwise of the education system used to measure political virility.

This is not to call for a return to the elitism of a former age. However, nearly 40 years on from the call for a 'great education debate', centralism is so taken for granted that governments can beat their breasts to claims that Ofsted is 'driving up standards'. Meanwhile, social divisions increase and children from economically deprived backgrounds achieve poorer comparative exam results; the gulf between them and their better-off peers continues to grow. Many parents have come to see, and a growing number of young people demonstrate daily, that the education system is not fit for purpose. In this, as in much else, evidence that the education agenda has brought any appreciable results is lacking. Such evidence as there is resembles nothing so much as the joke about the 'mad professor' who, having trained a spider to obey a series of movements on his command, pulled the legs off the creature and presented it as proof of his theory that a spider without legs is deaf!

The case presented in these opening paragraphs is, of course, luridly painted. In reality, individual teachers and individual inspectors remain, on the whole, humane people with a genuine interest in and concern for the development of young people. For Steiner Waldorf schools and early childhood settings, however, our distinctive approach poses problems for an inspectorate directed by public policy towards 'rigorous' standardisation and the blandishments of fickle fashions and assumed 'best practice'. Steiner educators fully accept the need for an inspectorate qualified to ensure that:

- The well-being and safety of young people is responsibly attended to both in terms of:

  —Premises, fixtures and fittings

  —School staff acting appropriately, with interests of learners paramount

- Schools receive objective appraisal that they are fulfilling their role effectively

- Parents and others receive a fair representation of what the school does

Steiner Waldorf educators work with a creative approach to teaching and a collaborative basis for management and leadership that aims to engender imagination, enthusiasm for lifelong learning and a strong sense of purpose in young people. The curriculum framework takes the development of the child as its starting point. Certain aspects of this—the later-than-usual start to academic education, the multidisciplinary Morning Lesson with its mix of music, movement, colour, form and narrative, the all-through, all-age nature of the educational approach and the collegial ethos that informs and sustains the teaching and management of the schools—make the Waldorf method significantly different to other main-tained or independent schools. These distinctive features are, of course, the reason parents choose

Steiner education. In many of the over 60 countries in which the schools are established they receive full or partial funding via the state. UK Steiner schools exist, albeit reluctantly, in the independent sector, this being the only way in which they have traditionally been able to sustain an approach and fundamental principles of an evolving education system that has proven effective over 80 years worldwide. The recent initiative to gain Academy status for one UK Waldorf school is an attempt to increase access to the education for a wider group of children, but this has been undertaken with a degree of wariness and concern for the compromises that may be entailed. Meanwhile, the piling up of government initiative upon initiative and continual tampering with the inspection system is an ever-present threat to the distinctiveness of all independent schools. More importantly, the way in which every school stands within the structures of state is being redefined and, in fact, regulation of the development of young people in general begins to look like a concerted campaign mounted to modify every molecule of childhood according to a prevailing set of social and economic assumptions. One might call this a process of 'memetic[1] modification' whose consequences are as uncertain, and potentially riskier, than their biological equivalent. Much more could be said about the issues around the regulation and inspection of early childhood settings, but, to avoid undue complications, we will concentrate here on the inspection of schools.[2]

Since the inspection model for independent schools was revised at the beginning of the 2000s, Steiner Waldorf Schools' Fellowship members have received generally good inspection reports, frequently indicating outstanding features (reports are available from the schools' and Ofsted websites). The majority of the lead inspectors were HMIs (employed directly by Ofsted), or retired HMIs with a strong sense of their prime directive, to inspect according to the aims and ethos of the school concerned, while upholding and evaluating compliance to essential regulations. Our schools have no problem at all with an inspectorate checking that regulations intended to ensure the well-being of young people are properly implemented. We also welcomed the introduction of the publication of reports (before 2001, these were held by Ofsted, but seen only by the school) and the clearer basis for inspection.

We note, however, that directly employed HMIs have increasingly become overseers of an inspection process which is politically directed. Although they continue to be involved in inspection visits, they work alongside a growing band of franchised regional and national inspection providers staffed by a mixture of former HMIs and AIs (additional inspectors, qualified to inspect, but not directly employed by Ofsted). Thus, currently, the Independent Schools' Council has their own inspection service (ISI), Focus Trust schools are inspected by School Inspection Services, with Bridge Trust expected soon to take up the inspection of certain independent religious and denominational schools. Cambridge Education, a large educational consultant and inspection provider, carries responsibility for the rest of the independent sector (Non-Association Independent schools). All providers have to follow the current Schedule 162a for inspections and visits lead to published reports. Schools pay for this privilege (up to a maximum of £10,000 for a school with 395 or more pupils), which, because school registration and inspection are compulsory, amounts to a further tax[3] on independent schools, whether they are profit-making or charitable. The inspection of maintained schools (so-called section 5 schedule inspections) is carried out by five Regional Inspection Service Providers (Nord Anglia Education PLC, CfBT, Cambridge Education Ltd, Prospectus, and Tribal Education Ltd). But the difference between the two inspection schedules appears to be eroding. Could there be a hidden motivation to encourage more independent schools into becoming Academies or Trust schools, or is the political agenda as lacking in reason or rationale as it often appears?

While Ofsted samples the inspections and reports of all the inspection providers, it acts essentially as a contractor. Ofsted's administrative and personnel basis, the directly employed school inspectors and support staff, has been shrinking while its role and responsibilities have grown. Thus, Steiner schools in England (in other parts of the UK the arrangements are different) have little to complain about so far. But there is a sense of unease at the way the inspection system, rather than depending on the educational judgement of committed inspectors, increasingly imposes a view of

101

education as quasi-management, assessed through tick-boxes and the distorting lens of dubious policy. Although we would not wish to impugn the integrity of any of the inspection providers, there must also be a question as to whether those inspection providers linked to large social and educational management consultancies, providing, for example, management of major social enterprise developments and steering the development of Academies, would be prepared to look critically at the way the Department for Children, Schools and Families determines how they should inspect. Especially so when the Ofsted quango simply flows in the incessant ooze of government policy, and has little choice but to do so. It is the nature of this governmental exuding and the apparent lack of self-reflective rigour in determining the basis for new policies that leaves schools at risk of falling into a morass not of their making. If, as expected, Ofsted is directed to include judgements on the effectiveness of 'leadership and management' of independent schools, the conflation and confusion between state provision and independent alternatives will be complete. Given the implicit assumptions and doubtful nature of such judgements, this is unlikely to benefit anyone, least of all children, who deserve to be taught by adults who lead from personal integrity and professional competence rather than at the hand of government-sponsored theory.

Educators such as the late Ted Wragg, Richard Pring, Michael Fielding, Chris McGovern and others have warned in their different ways of a dangerous retreat towards 'training' (essentially in the skills needed to succeed in the tests) and away from the rounded education that is the hallmark of civility. A comparable process has afflicted school inspections in England (less so, for example, in Wales). Educational 'delivery' has become the model for teaching; product sampling, that for inspection. But the social and democratic costs may be high: the instrumental systems of the State plant themselves within the classroom and stamp themselves all the more firmly on the communicative space in which young people are of necessity engaged in creating meaning and purpose for themselves. The invasion of Gog and Magog, those necessary but lumbering giant systems, Money and Power, into the meaning-sustaining, meaning-creating polity of democratic discourse has taken place with surprisingly little effective opposition, largely unobserved. Along with this, the dangers of top-down accountability, so ably critiqued in Onora O'Neil's Reith Lectures,[4] are manifest in many areas of public policy, especially education and health. Small surprise then that the summary of Anastasia de Waal's report for Civitas, *Inspection, Inspection, Inspection!*,[5] speaks of a climate of fear and impotence among schools with regard to the inspection system.

Rudolf Steiner, in the 1920s, foresaw a direction that was then evident most obviously in the experiments of Bolshevik Russia. He believed that without clear distinctions in the governance of cultural, political-rights and economic realms of society, economic-political demands would swamp education and increasingly marginalise every cultural activity. His reaction mirrors that of John Stuart Mill a generation before him.[6] In spite of the discrepancies between the blind drive of the education agenda and its manifestation, however, there are plenty of warning signs that the swarming initiatives carry disease, both social and academic: undermining teachers, increasing neurosis in young people and doing little to serve the needs of the economy, which is their apparent rationale in the first place.

Our unease grows as we follow the gradual convergence of maintained and independent school inspections. Although 'lighter touch' and less costly inspection visits are being introduced between the major six-yearly full inspections, the actual value of any of these as quality audits is being severely diminished by their reliance upon a School Information and Self-evaluation Form (SIEF). Even though the SIEF is not obligatory, any school not completing it is likely to be subject to a less favourable report. Thus, schools may be actively dissuaded from designing and sustaining their own specific forms of quality development appraisal. Although schools may add further information or provide details of their own appraisals to the SIEF, inspectors have decreasing time in which to refer to them and their record sheets are correspondingly limited. The policy pile has achieved the status of totem for inspectors. If something cannot be 'evidenced', it cannot be reported, but large areas of real educational activity may not show up because they do not appear in the inspection schedule. A few years before Ofsted was 'reformed', an inspector visiting a Steiner school was asked (and agreed) to give his report to the whole school community. In the presence of Chris Woodhead (just appointed HM Chief Inspector for Schools and visiting to experience how the inspection system was working), the inspector told the gathering: 'There is something I am not allowed to put in my report, but which has moved me during my visit: it is the quality of love I have experienced in the way the teachers and children work and learn together in this school.' The parent who reported this to me added that the Chief Inspector sat 'stony-faced'. There is far less room now for such observations, and the inspection system is the poorer for it. The education of children will not be better served by stony-faced expediency or by politically-corrected schools. Ofsted needs greater independence and inspectors need to become bold enough to state what they find on every level of experience, because growing and learning is not limited to tick-boxes.

Notes

Anastasia de Waal

1 Office for Standards in Education, Children's Services and Skills (Ofsted), 'Raising Standards, Improving Lives: The Office for Standards in Education, Children's Services and Skills Strategic Plan 2007-2010', October 2007.

2 Ofsted website, 'Working for Ofsted'; http://www.ofsted.gov.uk/Ofsted-home/About-us/Working-for-Ofsted

3 Bloom, A., *Times Educational Supplement*, 'Sats cause too much stress, say parents,' 12 September 2008, referring to a survey of over 100 parents by IVillage.

4 Paton, G., *Telegraph,* 'Ofsted: schools "teaching to the test"', 21 July 2008; *BBC News Online,* 'Too much maths "taught to the test"', 19 September 2008.

5 Ofsted, 'Focus on Improvement : proposals for maintained school inspections from September 2009', May 2008.

6 National Foundation of Educational Research, 'Impact of section 5 inspections: maintained schools in England', 2006.

7 David Bell, Teachernet discussion forum: 'Key Stage 2 framework for languages hotseat', 6 July 2005; http://www.teachernet.gov.uk/community/hotseats/ofsted/transcript/

8 David Bell, Teachernet discussion forum: 'Key Stage 2 framework for languages hotseat', 6 July 2005; http://www.teachernet.gov.uk/community/hotseats/ofsted/transcript/

9 'New inspection arrangements from September 2005—the story so far', Bristol local authority;

107

http://www.bristolcyps.org.uk/schools/improve/pdf/new_ofs ted_arrangements.pdf

10 Bubb, S. and Earley, P., 'The journey from self-evaluation to school improvement: the significance of effective profess-ional development', presented to the British Educational Leadership, Management and Administration Society's session 'Educational Leadership for the 21st Century: Creating our Future', American Educational Research Association Conference, New York, March 2008, p. 5.

11 Examples of private companies offering SEF consultancy include Baker-Philips, Maria Landy and Granada.

12 Tribal Education, Tribal Education Inspection Services, 'Briefing for Inspectors: frequently asked questions: what other work is available?', 2005.

13 Interview 15 July 2008.

14 See for example, Nord Anglia Plc, 'Outline Training Prog-ramme'; http://www.na-inspections.co.uk/training/new/

John MacBeath

1 The Standing International Conference of Central and General Inspectorates of Education (2004) Evaluation of schools providing Compulsory Education in Europe, 2004.

2 Cullingford, C. and Daniels, S., *The Effects of Ofsted Inspection on School Performance,* University of Huddersfield, 1998.

3 Woodhead, C., 'An Inspector responds', *Guardian Education,* 5 October 1999, p. 5.

4 Rosenthal, L., 'The cost of regulation in education: do school inspections improve school quality?', Department of Economics, University of Keele, 2001, p. 16.

5   Jones, S., Beale V., Kogan, M. and Maden, M., *The Ofsted System of School Inspection: an Independent Evaluation*, Centre for the Evaluation of Policy and Practice, Brunel University, 1999.

6   Dannawy, Y., 'Should we sugar coat the truth then miss?', Unpublished M.ED paper, Faculty of Education, University of Cambridge, 2001.

7   Dannawy, 'Should we sugar coat the truth then miss?', 2001.

8   MacBeath, J., *School Inspection and Self-evaluation*, London: Routledge, 2006, p. 30.

9   Matthews, P. and Sammons, P., 'Survival of the Weakest: the Differential Improvement of Schools Causing Concern in England, *London Review of Education*, Vol. 3, No. 4 (2), 159-176(18), 2005.

10 Ouston, J. and Davies, J. 'Ofsted and Afterwards: Schools' Responses to Inspection' in Earley, P. (ed.), *School Improvement after Ofsted Inspection: School and LEA Responses,* London: Sage Publications, 1998.

11 DfES, 'Personalised Learning: Building a New Relationship with Schools', speech by David Miliband, Minister of State for School Standards, North of England Conference, Belfast, 8 January 2004.

12 Leeuw, F., 'Reciprocity and the Evaluation of Educational Quality: Assumptions and Reality Checks', keynote paper for the European Union Congress, Karlstat, Sweden, 2-4 April 2001.

13 DfES, 'Personalised Learning', speech by David Miliband, 8 January 2004.

14 Ofsted, 'A New Relationship with Schools: Improving Performance Through Self-evaluation', 2005. (Emphasis in original.)

15 Tomkins, A., *School Administrator*, New York 1895 (4) quoted in Riley, K., *School Leadership and School Culture*, Washington: World Bank, 1998, p. 4.

16 See for examples Rosenholtz, S.J., *Teachers Workplace: The Social Organization of Schools*, New York: Teachers College, 1989; Stoll, L. and Myers, K., *No Quick Fixes: Perspectives on Schools in Difficulty*, London: Falmer Press, 1997; Gray, J. Hopkins, D., Reynolds, D., Wilcox, B., Farrell, S. and Jesson D., *Improving Schools: Performance and Potential*, Buckingham: Open University Press, 1999.

17 Parliamentary Select Committee on the work of Ofsted, 1999.

18 Elmore, R., *Agency, Reciprocity, and Accountability in Democratic Education,* Boston, Mass: Consortium for Policy Research in Education, 2005, p. 17.

Warwick Mansell

1   Taylor, M., in Yarnit, M. (ed.), *Advancing Opportunity: New Models of Schooling*, London: Smith Institute, 2007.

2   Robinson, S., *Times Educational Supplement*, 25 April 2008.

3   Ofsted statement to Warwick Mansell, 20 February 2008.

4   Wilde, S., Wright, S., Hayward, G., Johnson, J. and Sherett, R., 'Nuffield Review Higher Education Focus Groups Preliminary Report', 2005.

5　The Annual Report of Her Majesty's Chief Inspector of Schools 2004/05, *School Subject Report: English in Secondary Schools;* http://live.ofsted.gov.uk/publications/annualreport0405/4.2.5.html

6　Collins, S., Reiss, M. and Stobart, G., *The Effects of National Testing in Science at Key Stage 2 in England and Wales*, Institute of Education, University of London, 2008.

Mick Brookes

1　Mansell, W., *Education by Numbers: The Tyranny of Testing*, London: Politicos, 2007.

2　Education Data Surveys; http://www.educationdatasurveys.org.uk

Kevin Avison

1　Memetic/meme—a word coined by Richard Dawkins to denote the cultural equivalent of a gene.

2　Since April 2007, Ofsted has become a 'super-regulator' for children and learners of all ages, its remit now running right across the spectrum of education in all its forms.

3　The proposed introduction of an annual charging system, though welcome from the point of view of schools setting budgets, confirms the impression that the charges are a form of taxation.

4　O'Neill, O., *A Question of Trust*, BBC Reith Lectures, 2002.

5　de Waal, A, *Inspection, Inspection, Inspection! How Ofsted Crushes Independent Schools and Independent Teachers*, London: Civitas, 2006.

6   Mill, J.S., *On Liberty*: 'A general State education is a mere
    contrivance for moulding people to be exactly like one
    another: and as the mould in which it casts them is that
    which pleases the predominant power in the government,
    whether this be a monarch, a priesthood, an aristocracy, or
    the majority of the existing generation; in proportion as it is
    efficient and successful, it establishes a despotism over the
    mind, leading by natural tendency to one over the body.'
    p. 239.